Your Classroom Library

New Ways to Give It More Teaching Power

Great Teacher-Tested
and Research-Based Strategies for
Organizing and Using Your Library to Increase
Students' Reading Achievement

BY D. RAY REUTZEL AND PARKER C. FAWSON

SCHOLASTIC
PROFESSIONAL BOOKS

NEW YORK • TORONTO • LONDON • AUCKLAND • SYDNEY
MEXICO CITY • NEW DELHI • HONG KONG • BUENOS AIRES

Dedications

To the many teachers who continue to inspire me with their unflagging commitment to children and schools, I express my deepest appreciation. I thank you who have taught my five children during the past twenty years and you who will yet teach my children and grandchildren

To my wife Pam, who is herself a wonderfully effective teacher, an exemplary mother, and my dearest and truest friend in this life and beyond.

To my five wonderful children, Chris, Jeremy, Candice, Cody, and Austin, and to my three grandchildren, Dylan, Denver, and Carter, who continue to inspire my love for education and the hope that all children everywhere will have equal access to excellent educational opportunities. —RR

To my wife Debra, who has inspired me with her honesty and love for learning. Her support and encouragement to complete this book have been deeply appreciated. She is my inspiration and most cherished friend.

To our five amazing children, who add meaning and focus to life.

To the many children, teachers, and colleagues who have expanded my understanding of the powerful influence of context on reading success. —PCF

Acknowledgments

This book began years ago with a group of graduate students, teachers, administrators, and children. After many hours observing the "library period" in schools, we determined that this educational experience was undernourished and only haphazardly connected to a school's literacy program. We conducted research to understand how children select books and how teachers construct and maintain classroom libraries.

To the faculties and administrators of Sage Creek, Grant, and Art City Elementary Schools in Springville, Utah, we say thank you for helping us take this journey into classroom libraries. To the teachers in these schools and many others in central Utah, in Alpine, Jordan, Nebo, and Provo school districts, we express gratitude for offering ideas, opening classrooms for photographs, and making suggestions on the "drafty" stages of this book. And to the students who taught us so much as we sat in on their classes, we express our thanks. We couldn't have done it without all of these wonderful people.

To Merryl Maleska Wilbur, our editor, we offer our gratitude for keeping us on schedule, for offering needed encouragement, for making our book speak with a singular voice and power, and for giving freely of her talents. She was consistently pleasant and very meticulous in her work.

To Wendy Murray and Terry Cooper, we express our gratitude for giving us a chance to share our insights with teachers through the effective network of professional books published by Scholastic. Without their faith and vision, this book would never have been.

To Jackie Swensen, the book designer, we express thanks for capturing graphically the spirit of our message and for attending to hundreds of details in a timely, efficient manner.

We have enjoyed the opportunity as colleagues to learn from one another in the writing of this book. It has been one more trip down a long and continuing road as colleagues and friends.

Thanks to the students and teachers whose work appears in this book.
Special thanks to Judy Freeman, Diane Miness, and Jean Turner who have each contributed
unique insights and ideas; their contributions are noted individually within the book.

Cover design by Jim Sarfati
Cover photo by Mike Snelson
Interior design by Solutions by Design, Inc.
Interior photos courtesy of the authors

ISBN 0-439-26082-5

Table of Contents

How Does the Classroom Library Support Reading *to* Children?

How Does the Classroom Library Support Reading *With* Children?

CHAPTER 1

Creating and Sustaining an Effective Classroom Library

Ms. Nelson moves to her familiar place in the rocking chair in the corner of the classroom, where each day she reads aloud from a new book. Today's book is *My Little Sister Ate One Hare* (Grossman, 1996). The first graders are excitedly settling in on a large, comfy rug for today's Read Aloud time. Ms. Nelson shows them the cover of the book and asks, "What do you see?" Jon pipes up quickly, "Hey, that girl is juggling a bunny rabbit! It looks like she's gonna eat it." "Good observation, Jon. Let's read the title together." The children and Ms. Nelson read aloud, "My Little Sister Ate One Hare." "Does anyone know what the word *hare* means?" inquires Ms. Nelson. "I do, I do!" giggles Melinda. "It means the stuff on your head, arms, and legs." "Yes," Ms. Nelson comments, "that is one meaning of the word. Now look up at the board. Let me

write the word *hair* that Melinda is talking about. Do these two words, *hare* and *hair*, look the same? How are they different?" The children discuss the differences, and Micha guesses that the word *hare* is another word for bunny or rabbit. "That's correct, Micha," replies Ms. Nelson.

After more discussion about the cover, Ms. Nelson enthusiastically reads the book aloud to the children. As the children pick up on the patterns of the text, they begin to spontaneously laugh and comment on it. After discussing the book, they reread it, using their fingers to count.

When they are finished, Ms. Nelson places the book in a display rack in her classroom library. She tells the children: "Remember, this book is in the class library if you want to read it to yourself or someone else."

Ms. Nelson's classroom library is filled with many kinds of reading and writing materials and is thoughtfully organized to make these varied materials accessible to children for their exploration and learning. Like any good classroom library, it is a purposefully arranged, carefully planned permanent space in which a variety of reading and writing materials are stored and displayed.

Think of it this way—a classroom library is to a balanced reading and writing program what a kitchen is to a home. The classroom library is the place where the ingredients are assembled so that people can come together to treat themselves to a rich variety of literary genres. Classroom libraries, like kitchens, provide staple foods (the core book collection), along with exciting new recipes (books that come and go). Classroom libraries, like kitchens, also provide for dining in or take-out. Students can read onsite, check out books, trade them with friends, or place book orders.

Classroom libraries should be more than a haphazard collection of donated books, sale books, or those earned with class book-order points. The classroom library can be seen as the organizational hub around which a balanced and comprehensive instructional program is arranged. If the classroom library is adequately provisioned, thoughtfully put together, and interactively used, it will form the foundation for literacy success (Neuman, 1999).

The Growing Importance of the Classroom Library

The school library has traditionally been the centralized gatekeeper of literature for students. Many of us recall the weekly march to the school library, where we were allowed to browse rows and rows of books and magazines. It was an event keenly anticipated. In the earliest grades, we located our favorite authors on shelves filled with easy-to-read picture books. We also looked for the books our teacher had read to us, but these were often the first to be checked out. When we were a bit older, we sometimes checked out the book the teacher was reading in class so that we could follow along. We rushed with hopeful anticipation to the shelf containing series books to catch up on the latest antics of our favorite characters. Some of us selected magazines to read up on our latest hobbies or interests.

The librarian usually read a new book to us and followed this reading with brief instructions on how to find different kinds of books in the library. Quite frankly, the visit to the school library was one of the few opportunities we had as students to explore our own interests free from the academic constraints of the classroom.

Little had changed from the time we were children to when we began our teaching careers several decades ago. The school library was and far too often still is merely a weekly experience for both student and teacher. In the 1960s and early '70s, curriculums began to demand that students have ready access to hands-on learning and information to support intellectual and social growth (Brown, 1978). However, at the same time, the student population in many schools was expanding beyond available resources. This increase meant that children's access to print resources in the school library was curtailed. The weekly visit to the library, which already had been only minimally effective in supporting student interest and learning, now was often limited to even fewer visits. Even worse, budget limitations constricted the purchasing of new print and media materials in school libraries during this period of student population growth.

The '80s and '90s brought vast changes in our understanding of literacy learning. The

TEACHING IN ACTION: *The Grand Opening*

As a first-grade teacher, the focal point of my classroom is our class library. From the first day of school, everything we do is linked in some way to that "magical space." Our library includes many shelves of books, the majority of which are arranged A–Z with separate sections for holiday books, bear books, Dr. Seuss books, poetry books, ABC books, I Can Read books, Magic Tree House books, and a variety of other "themed" or author-based sections.

I do not open the complete library to students during the first weeks of school; instead, I open it gradually in stages. This builds a wonderful sense of excitement and anticipation among the children. It would be overwhelming (and not very practical) to have children select books from the library as soon as school begins. So for the first few weeks, we work as a group to develop class guidelines on book handling and care of books; to learn how the library is organized so we can find what we need or want; and to learn what kinds of books we have in our classroom. We also learn to use "bookfinders," which are special plastic markers that "hold a place" on the shelf and remind children where to return their book if they've forgotten our ABC order rule.

During these early weeks, students are able to use books that are set up in different areas of the classroom. Since we have such a large classroom library, books are displayed all over the room—in tubs or containers and on smaller bookshelves and in book wedges (see photo on page 26). The book wedges, which display books face front so that

children can see the covers, are organized by beginning-of-the-year themes such as ABC books, family books (our first social studies unit), rocks/sand/soil books (our first science unit), fall stories, and so on. The children select from these wedges throughout the day for quiet reading activities or investigations. In addition to all these books, there are color tubs of leveled books on top of our library shelves. These books are available to children after approximately the first three weeks of school.

While all this is going on, there is a big sign up in the actual shelf area that says: *These Library Shelves Are Closed!*

The day we open the shelves, we hold a little ceremony. As the sign comes down, there is fanfare with music. This is an exciting and much-anticipated moment: Our classroom library is officially open!

— Diane Miness, first-grade teacher, Dutch Neck School, Princeton Junction, NJ whole language movement, which emphasized authentic reading, grew rapidly. Soon both researchers and classroom teachers were exploring literature-based teaching; real literature, often in the form of trade books, assumed a central role in the teaching of reading. By the '90s, with the advent of the technology revolution, it became clear that classrooms needed more, not less, print information available for children and teachers.

As a result, many teachers began to recognize the need to establish their own classroom libraries complete with the requisite, contemporary information technology. Today, more than ever, we have come to recognize how important it is for students to be read to, to collaborate in their reading with others, and to have opportunities to read a wide variety of texts independently. Research has demonstrated time and again the correlation between the amount students read and their reading achievement (Allington, 2001). With all this in mind, we can no longer rely solely upon a weekly or bi-monthly visit to the school library to support comprehensive literacy instruction.

As you read this book, we encourage you to think of the library in your room as the *heart* of effective literacy instruction. Teachers who have developed and organized their own classroom libraries are not only able to use print and electronic media to support the curriculum and students' learning interests, they are also better able to select materials for inclusion in the classroom library. This means, in turn, that students have greater access to a variety of narrative and expository materials to read with others and on their own. In the remainder of this chapter we discuss the centrality of the classroom library in providing children with effective, balanced, and comprehensive reading and writing instruction.

The Place of a Classroom Library in a Balanced Reading Program

Every day in a balanced reading program, teachers read *to* children. As we explore in Chapter 3, they do this to model for children how expressive and fluent oral reading can sound. They do this to expose children to the wide variety of reading materials available to both the avid and the reluctant reader. And they do this to help children connect with the emotions, events, and information found in books, and thus encourage them to make reading a part of their lives.

Every day in a balanced reading program, as we'll see in Chapter 4, teachers read *with* their students. They do this to guide, shape, and direct their students' development of effective reading strategies and skills. They do this to show children how to sustain their reading progress and extend their thoughts with books. They do this to model for students how to read as writers, how to use literary craft techniques such as developing an author voice. And they do this to create a sense of community in the classroom both by sharing a book with the entire class and in small groups.

Every day in a balanced reading program, teachers create the conditions and provide time for reading *by* the children on their own. As Chapter 5 explains, they do this because they understand that children learn to read by reading. They do this because they know that to become lifelong readers, children need to become comfortable with choosing their own books. They do this because students need large amounts of daily time spent reading to get good at reading.

On the next page is a chart of the key elements of a successful literacy instruction program. Keep this chart in mind as you read the rest of this book. Think of it as a blueprint for the book and try to fill in the right-hand column with additional ideas as you read subsequent chapters.

Five Major Functions of the Classroom Library

If you think of a classroom library as a cozy, welcoming space where students can read quietly or browse through a rich collection of texts, you are only partially correct. The fact that classroom libraries are places for storage and quiet is only one small part of their purpose. They are, in the broadest sense, the backbone of classroom activity: Much of what goes on each day draws from or occurs in or around the resources and space within the classroom library.

As we see it, there are at least five important functions of an effectively designed classroom library.

A good classroom library helps students locate books easily and gives them room to get comfortable.

1. Supporting Literacy Instruction

The first function of a classroom library is to support reading and writing instruction—in school and out. To this end, outfit your classroom library with books and other media materials to support student learning in all of the daily curriculum subjects. Include materials related to science, health, mathematics, history, economics, geography, music, art, drama, dance, languages, grammar, spelling, literature, computers, and other topics. Build an adequate collection of fiction and nonfiction materials at enough different levels to accommodate the many interests and abilities of students desiring to check out books for take-home reading. (See page Chapter 2, page 45, for a specific suggestion about setting up a check-out system that also motivates readers.)

An abundant collection of both nonfiction and fiction meets varied student interests.

Elements of a Balanced Reading and Writing Program and Their Relationship to the Classroom Library

A Balanced Literacy Program Means:	The Classroom Library Supports and Extends These Goals By:
Reading and Writing TO Children	❖ Read Alouds ❖ Trade books of many genres & levels ❖ Comfortable rug space, rocking chair ❖ _____
Reading and Writing WITH Children	❖ Modeling ❖ Book talks ❖ Live interviews ❖ Guided reading ❖ _____
Reading and Writing BY Children	❖ Large collection of various materials ❖ Children's own writing housed side-by-side with published books ❖ _____
Creating and Sustaining an Enriched Literacy Classroom	❖ Books talks and "openings" ❖ Readers' Theater ❖ Students job assignments such as "class librarian" ❖ Book Reviews and reports displayed ❖ _____
Providing Integrated, Intentional, Explicit Skill Instruction	❖ Mini-lessons on relevant skills using library books ❖ Books that can be used to highlight skills recently taught ❖ _____
Connecting the Home and School Effectively	❖ Books read at home recorded on charts ❖ Parent volunteers involved ❖ _____
Informing Instruction With Assessment	❖ Natural spot for teacher observation of reading behaviors ❖ Teacher-student reading conferences ❖ _____
Offering a Comprehensive Curriculum Scope and Sequence	❖ Learning center for cross-curricular studies, with content area titles housed here ❖ Instructional extension of the reading program ❖ _____
Using a Variety of Grouping Strategies	❖ Leveled books ❖ Text sets ❖ Inviting place for "early finishers" and the "temporarily overwhelmed" ❖ _____
Adapting Instruction for Learners With Special Needs	❖ Leveled books ❖ _____
Supplying Students With a Variety of Reading and Writing Texts	❖ The "kid-friendly" home for these texts ❖ Area for ordering new books, best books lists, book advertisements ❖ _____

2. Helping Students to Learn About Books

Next, an effective classroom library provides a place for teachers to teach and children to learn about books and book selection. Here children can experience a variety of book genres and other reading materials in a smaller and more controlled environment than in the school or public library. You can also use the classroom library to teach students how to take care of books. You can set up a book repair area for instruction on repair, and display a poster with clear directions on how to mend torn pages, remove marks in the books, cover frayed edges, or fix broken bindings.

You can also use the classroom library to teach students effective strategies for selecting relevant, interesting, and appropriate reading materials (see pages 49–51 for model lessons on this). As the quote (Timion, 1992) below expresses, many students do not have adequate, flexible strategies for selecting appropriate reading materials. In fact, to let your students know that you understand this challenge, you might consider creating a banner for your library as demonstrated here.

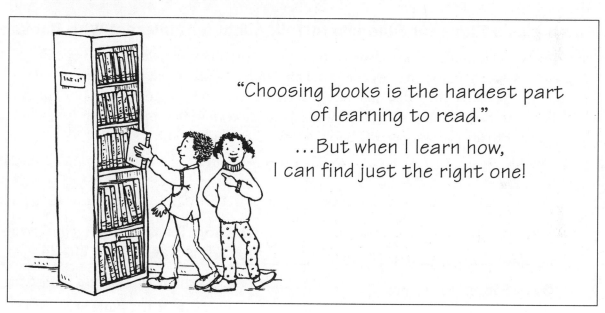

"Choosing books is the hardest part of learning to read."

...But when I learn how, I can find just the right one!

You might extend this strategy instruction by applying it to the school or public library, showing students how they can locate books of interest in these larger settings. And, very important as well, you can help them learn to navigate the Internet in order to locate information about specific books or choices for reading material.

3. Providing a Central Location for Classroom Resources

You can also use your classroom library as an organized central storage location for classroom instructional resources. Here is additional space for organizing science equipment, CD and tape players, VHS and DVD tapes, computers wired to the Internet, games, magazines, and other materials that support learning. In this respect, the classroom library mirrors the organization of media centers at the individual and district levels.

4. Providing Opportunities for Independent Reading and Curricular Extensions

The fourth important function of a classroom library is as a resource and location for independent reading, personal exploration, project research, and individual assessment. Every good comprehensive reading program provides students daily time to read independently. The classroom library is typically the resource that supports children's daily independent reading of self-selected books that meet their personal, recreational reading interests. The classroom library also provides students with readily accessible print materials, expository books, computer technology, and media for conducting research or completing curricular extension projects.

Further, an in-class library offers a setting for students to quietly read aloud and discuss a book with a peer or the teacher. This provides an ideal opportunity for you to conduct an informal assessment of each student's reading, which will help you to plan individualized instruction.

5. Serving as a Place for Students to Talk About and Interact With Books

The effective classroom library also functions as a gathering spot where students and teachers can express their lives as readers. Think of it as a place that makes books exciting, that sells reading. It should be a place students can't wait to get to. Here they can talk about their reactions to books, write a critical review and share it with peers, or draw a poster to advertise a favorite book. A few other ideas follow:

✺ The library can be a place where students contribute to a list of "The Top Ten Books This Week in [——] Grade."

The Top Ten Books in Second Grade This Week: October 10–14
Owen Foote, Money Man
Back to the Blue
Hooray for Diffendoofer Day
Alexander Who Used to Be Rich Last Sunday
A Job for Wittilda
Virgie Goes to School With Us Boys
The Seven Eaters
Amelia and Eleanor Go for a Ride
Big Moon Tortilla
Annie and the Old One

The Top Ten Books in Fifth Grade This Week: April 20–24
There's a Boy in the Girl's Bathroom
The Case of the Muttering Mummy
Holes
Salamandastron
Guinness World Records
Bunnicula: A Rabbit-Tale of Mystery
The Eyes of the Killer Robot
Captain Underpants and the Wrath of the Wicked Wedgie Woman
Eyewitness Book: World War II
The Black Stallion Returns

- ❋ It may also be a place where students can advertise a "book swap" with other students.

- ❋ It can be a place where students plan a dramatization of a book with a small group of peers.

Students advertise books they would like to swap.

Dramatizing Books Gets Readers Hooked

To get readers to live a book, and not just read the words, incorporate creative drama and Readers' Theater into your classroom library routines. For each of these activities, the classroom library provides both a stage for practice and performance and a central storage spot for the books themselves.

Particularly zesty, lively scenes work best. For example, *Hilary and the Troublemakers* by Kathleen Leverich (Greenwillow, 1992) has a dramatic chapter, ideal for third or fourth graders to act out: Hilary comes to school and tells her class and her disbelieving teacher that a giant owl has eaten her math homework ("Fractions," he says, "my favorite!").

For first graders, scenes from Peggy Rathmann's *Officer Buckle and Gloria* (Putnam, 1995)—where police dog Gloria dramatizes Officer Buckle's boring safety tips lectures behind his back and without his knowledge—are bound to bring giggles and fun.

All grades love to bring Aesop's *Fables* to life. Read aloud a selection of well-known and lesser-known fables. Break your class into groups. Have each group individually rehearse its fable and then perform it for the rest of the class. Or do an all-class production of "The Boy Who Cried Wolf," which has an unlimited cast of villagers and sheep.

Readers' Theater encourages children to read aloud with expression, comprehension, and fluency, and to walk in a character's shoes. For quick and easy Readers' Theater material, look for picture books with plenty of action, humor, characters, and narration. Easy readers, such as Arnold Lobel's Frog and Toad series or Cynthia Rylant's *Poppleton, Mr. Putter and Tabby* or her Henry and Mudge books, have short, self-contained chapters that are often perfect to copy, hand out to groups of readers, and have them perform aloud in character. You can write up a script, or have your students create the script.

—Ideas provided by Judy Freeman, children's literature consultant, *Book Talk* columnist for *Instructor* magazine, and author of *More Books Kids will Sit Still For* (Bowker/Greenwood, 1995)

Planning Your Classroom Library

Classroom libraries come in all shapes and sizes. Our experiences in planning an effective classroom library as well as those of others (Fractor, Woodruff, Martinez, and Teale, 1993) reveal at least three major considerations: 1) the nature of the collection; 2) the size of the collection; and 3) how you use the collection for responses to reading.

Determine the Nature of the Collection

As you plan for your classroom library, you need to remember that it will be supporting and inviting students of many different abilities to engage in reading a variety of texts, both narrative and expository (Burke, 2000; Report of the National Reading Panel National Institute of Health, 2000; Allington, 2001). Each text type requires a reader to use different strategies. Expository texts require that students gather and organize facts, as well as critically analyze information. Narrative texts invite students to connect with personal experiences and empathize with the characters in a book. Since students should read a variety of text types, we have developed the list at right of varied reading materials to be considered for inclusion in a classroom library.

Classroom libraries should also house a collection of leveled text materials, both narrative and expository, for meeting students' instructional needs. Sufficient quantities of high-interest, leveled books need to be available to comply with the "Goldilocks principle" of achieving a "just right" match between the challenges within the text and each student's interests and needs (Ohlhausen and Jepsen, 1992).

Recommended Categories of Reading Materials for a Classroom Library

- ❉ Textbooks, including the classroom basal readers
- ❉ Computers with bookmarked Web pages, including those of the National Archives, the Library of Congress, and other major reference sources
- ❉ Stories and narrative accounts, e.g., fairy tales, folk tales, and biographies
- ❉ Picture books with thought-provoking images and unique examples of artistic talent
- ❉ Tests, quizzes, and worksheets for "test prep"
- ❉ Miscellaneous reading materials, such as popular magazines, newspapers, catalogs, recipe books, encyclopedias, greeting cards, maps, telephone books, reports, captioned photographs, posters, diaries, and letters
- ❉ Joke books, comic books, word-puzzle books, and so forth
- ❉ Essays, editorials, and critiques
- ❉ Student-authored books and stories
- ❉ Leveled stories, decodable books, pattern books, and predictable books

Establish the Size of the Collection

The size of the collection depends upon how much monetary support is available in your school and upon how much creativity and energy you can bring to the task. Very often, organizing an effective classroom library requires a multi-year, phase-in plan. Resources are seldom sufficient to immediately provision a classroom library adequately. (One thing you might consider is helping your school apply for a grant. *Get a Grant! Yes You Can!* (Scholastic, 1998) might be a good initial source of information.)

Also, the size of the collection varies with its functions in and out of the classroom as determined in the plan. If, for example, the classroom library exists primarily or exclusively to service students' independent reading selections, then the library collection may include 10 to 12 titles per student (Veatch, 1968; Neuman, 2000). This means that if a teacher has 30 children in her classroom, an adequate library for independent reading would be between 300 and 350 book titles. On the other hand, if the

Recommended Size Ranges for a Library Collection of 300–375 Titles

- ❋ Poetry collections: 3-5 titles
- ❋ Pattern/predictable books: 50-60 titles
- ❋ Leveled books: 120-140 titles
- ❋ Decodable books: 40-50 titles
- ❋ Information books: 40-50 titles
- ❋ Award-winning books: 30-40 titles
- ❋ Reference books such as dictionaries (5-10), thesauri (1-2), CD-ROM encyclopedias (1-2 disks), and atlases (1-2)
- ❋ Newspapers (1-2 subscriptions), magazines (1-3 subscriptions), recipe books (1-3), and catalogs (3-4)
- ❋ Series books: 3-4 series
- ❋ Scripts for plays, skits, and Readers Theater: 1-3 titles

teacher intends to use the classroom library to support cross-curricular studies, take-home reading, guided reading, shared reading, reading aloud, and professional development for the teacher, the size of the classroom library collection may range from 1,500 to 2,000 titles, including many multiple copies. Below, we recommend size ranges that would provide a varied selection for a minimum classroom library collection of 300 to 375 titles.

Build Your Collection

It is one thing to establish the size limits of your classroom library. It is quite another to actually build your collection. In order to help you get started, we offer here one list of recommended titles for the primary grades and another for the intermediate grades. Each of these lists is based on the categories we presented on page 16. As you look over these lists, keep in mind two important points. These titles represent our own recommendations; there are many other excellent titles out there. Also, they represent only a small portion of the numbers of books a good classroom library should include. But at least these lists should provide you with a start.

Some Recommended Books for Grades K-2

POETRY

A Treasury of Mother Goose Rhymes, Publications International Limited
A Light in the Attic, Shel Silverstein
A New Kid on the Block, Jack Prelutsky

PATTERN/PREDICTABLE BOOKS

The Carrot Seed, Ruth Krauss
We Like Fruit, Millen Lee
I Can See, Adria Klein
I Like, Gay Su Pinnell
A Party, Joy Cowley
The Ghost, Joy Cowley
Lunch at the Zoo, Wendy Blaxland
How Many Fish, Rachel Gossett and Margaret Ballinger
Dan the Flying Man, Joy Cowley
Is it Time? Jane Campbell
Jump Rope, Claudette C. Mitchell, Gracie R. Porter, and Patricia T. Cousin
Monkey See, Monkey Do, Marc Gane
Itchy, Itchy Chicken Pox, Grace Maccarone
My Friends, Taro Gomi
Buzz Said the Bee, Wendy C. Lewison
More Spaghetti I Say, Rita G. Gelman
Noisy Nora, Rosemary Wells
The Little Mouse, the Red Ripe Strawberry, and the

Big Hungry Bear, Don and Audrey Wood
Knots on a Counting Rope, Bill Martin Jr. and Don Archambault
Chicka, Chicka, Boom, Boom, Bill Martin Jr. and Don Archambault
This Is the Place for Me, Joanna Cole
Mr. McCready's Cleaning Day, Tracey Shilling

LEVELED BOOKS

A

Underwater, Rebel Williams
I Like to Find Things, Gavin Bishop
Dogs, Amy Levin
Painting, Joy Cowley
Moms & Dads, Beverly Randell, Jenny Giles, and Annette Smith

B

Hats Around the World, Liza Charlesworth
Making Mountains, Margaret Ballinger and Rachel Gossett
For Breakfast, Patricia T. Cousin, Claudette C. Mitchell, and Gracie R. Porter
Here I Am, Judy Nayer
Sally's New Shoes, Annette Smith

C

At the Store, Patricia T. Cousin, Claudette C.
    Mitchell, and Gracie R. Porter
One for You and One for Me, Wendy Blaxland
In the City, Susan Pasternac
Bo and Peter, Betsy Franco
Fishing, Annette Smith

D

The Ball Game, David Packard
Hide and Seek, Roberta Brown and Sue Carey
Where We Live, Brenda Parkes
The Farm Concert, Joy Cowley
Lizard Loses Its Tail, Beverly Randell

E

The Rain and the Sun, Allan Trussell-Cullen
Which Hat Today, Margaret Ballinger and Rachel
    Gossett
The Red Rose, Joy Cowley
My Dad's Truck, Meredith Costain
Tortillas, Margarita Gonzelez-Jensen

F

My Very Hungry Pet, Debbie Swan
The Best Thing About Food, Fay Robinson
The Jigaree, Joy Cowley
Late for Soccer, Jeremy Giles
Tabby in the Tree, Beverly Randell

G

Knobby Knuckles, Knobby Knees, Jill Carter and
    Judy Ling
How Have I Grown, Mary Reid
Balcony Garden, Rebecca Weber
Grandpa's Lemonade, Helen Upson
William's Skateboard, Dale Golder

H

Mom's Secret, Meredith Costain
I Was Walking Down the Road, Sarah Barchas
Digging to China, Kathern Goldsby
Robert and the Rocket, Leesa Waldron
George Shrinks, William Noyce

I

Dancin' Down, Evageline Nicholas
The Friendly Crocodile, Monica Hiris
Swimming Lessons, Amy Algie
Big Bad Rex, Betty Erickson

The Witch's Haircut, Mavis Wyvill

J

Stone Soup, Ann McGovern
Dolphins, Marion Rego
There's an Alligator Under My Bed, Mercer Mayer
King Midas and the Golden Touch, Allan
    Trussell-Cullen
Children of Sierra Leone, Arma Christiana

DECODABLE BOOKS

Sam and Tat, Jane Dude
Dan and the Fan, Jane Dude
A Hat for Nan, Jane Dude
Jog to the Dam, Annette Williams
Tam on Sam, Annette Williams
Tall in the Saddle, Argentina Palacios
The Internet: A Kid's Handbook, Francie Alexander
    and Nancy Hechinger
Todd's Journal, Kana Riley
The Cat in the Hat, Dr. Seuss
Green Eggs and Ham, Dr. Seuss
In My Bed, Ron Bacon

NONFICTION, INFORMATION BOOKS

What Do Insects Do? Susan Canizares and Pamela
    Chanko
Monkeys, Susan Canizares and Pamela Chanko
At the Zoo, Beverly Randell, Jenny Giles, and
    Annette Smith
Who Lives in the Arctic? Susan Canizares and
    Pamela Chanko
Who Lives in a Tree? Susan Canizares and Daniel
    Moreton
Moving, Peter and Sheryl Sloan
Hair, Jackie Carter
City Signs, Brenda Parkes
Weather, Pamela Chanko and Daniel Moreton
At Work, Margaret Mooney
My Flag, Brenda Parkes
Over the Oregon Trail, Rita Ramsted
What Lays Eggs? Katherine Grace Stone
Brave Triceratops, Beverly Randell
Stamps, John Parsons
Tides, Eva Petro
Go to the Hospital, Sandra Iversen
Coral, Stanley L. Swartz
Insects, Carolyn MacLulich,
What Do Zoo Keepers Do? Jungle Jack Hanna
A Book About Your Skeleton, Ruth Belov Gross

Louis Braille, Margaret Davidson
Dolphin's First Day, Kathleen W. Zoehfeld

SERIES BOOKS

Woodland Mystery Series, Irene Schultz
June B. Jones, Barbara Park
Frog & Toad, Arnold Lobel
Cam Jansen Mysteries, David A. Adler
The Berenstain Bears, Stan and Jan Berenstain
The Adventures of the Bailey School Kids, Debbie
    Dadey and Marcia Thornton Jones

AWARD WINNERS

Have You Seen My Ducklings?, Nancy Tafuri
Uncle Jed's Barbershop, Margaree King Mitchell
May I Bring a Friend?, Beatrice S. DeRegniers
Seven Blind Mice, Ed Young
Miss Rumphius, Barbara Cooney
When I Was Young in the Mountains, Cynthia Rylant
A Visit to William Blake's Inn, Alice and Martin
    Provensen
Song and Dance Man, Karen Ackerman
Make Way for Ducklings, Robert McCloskey
The Biggest Bear, Lynd Ward
Madeline's Rescue, Ludwig Bemelman
The Snowy Day, Ezra Jack Keats
Sam, Bangs, and Moonshine, Evaline Ness
Jumanji, Chris Van Alsburg
Smoky Night, Eve Bunting
Joseph Had a Little Coat, Simms Tabak

MAGAZINES

U.S. Kids
Ranger Rick
National Geographic World
Nickelodeon

RECIPE BOOKS

Betty Crocker
Martha Stewart Living Cookbook
Cooking for Dummies

CATALOGS

Clothing
Pet supplies
Toys

READERS THEATER SCRIPTS

http://www.geocities.com/Athens/Thebes/9893
    /readerstheater.htm
http://falcon.jmu.edu/~ramseyil/readersmine.htm

DICTIONARIES

Macmillan Picture Dictionary for Children,
    Robert Costello
Scholastic Visual Dictionary, Jean Claude Corbeil
    and Ariane Archambault
The Oxford Picture Dictionary, Norma Shapiro and
    Jayme Adelson-Goldstein

ATLASES

World Book Atlas, World Book
Complete Atlas of the World, Raintree Steck-Vaughn
U.S. Atlas for Young People, Kathie Billingslea Smith

THESAURUSES AND SPELLERS

How to Spell It, Harriet Wittles and Joan Greisman
The Clear and Simple Thesaurus, Grossett and
    Dunlap

CD-ROM ENCYCLOPEDIAS

Encarta
Encyclopedia Britannica

ENCYCLOPEDIAS

Picture Encyclopedia for Children, Grosset and
    Dunlap
Children's First Encyclopedia, Dempsey Parr
    Publishers

Some Recommended Books for Grades 3–6

POETRY

Where the Sidewalk Ends, Shel Silverstein
A Pizza the Size of the Sun, Jack Prelutsky

LEVELED BOOKS

K

Buffalo Bill and the Pony Express, Elenor Coerr
Keep the Lights Burning, Abbie, Peter and Connie Roop
More Tales of Oliver Pig, Jean V. Leeuwen
Nate the Great Goes Undercover, Marjorie W. Sharmat

L

Happy Birthday, Martin Luther King, Jean Marzollo
Katy and the Big Snow, Virginia L. Burton
The Littles, John Peterson
Teach Us, Amelia Bedelia, Peggy Parish

M

Amazing Grace, Mary Hoffman and Caroline Binch
Blueberries for Sal, Robert McCloskey
Cloudy With a Chance of Meatballs, Judi Barrett
Kate Shelley and the Midnight Express, Margaret K. Wetterer

N

Rumpelstiltskin, Paul O. Zelinsky
Lion Dance, Kate Waters and Madeline Slovenz-Low
The Most Wonderful Doll in the World, Phyllis McGinley
We'll Never Forget You, Roberto Clemente, Trudie Engel

O

Gladly Here I Come, Joy Cowley
The Mouse and the Motorcycle, Beverly Cleary
The Bad Dad List, Anna Kenna
The Sock Gobbler and Other Stories, Barbara Berge

P

The T.F. Letters, Karen Ray
A Taste of Blackberries, Doris B. George
The Private Notebook of Katie Roberts, Sonja Lamut
Justin and the Best Biscuits in the World, Mildred P. Walter

Q

Run Away from Home, Patricia C. McKissack
The Great Brain Does It Again, John D. Fitzgerald

Sara Crewe, Frances H. Burnett
The Story of George Washington Carver, Eva Moore

R

Fourth Grade Rats, Jerry Spinelli
Sounder, William Armstrong
The Best, Worst School Year Ever, Barbara Robinson
The Story of Thomas Alva Edison: The Wizard of Menlo Park, Margaret Davidson

S

There's a Boy in the Girls Bathroom, Louis Sacher
Little House on the Prairie, Laura I. Wilder
Stone Fox, John R. Gardiner
The Great Gilly Hopkins, Katherine Paterson

T

The Chronicles of Narnia, C. S. Lewis
Old Yeller, Fred Gipson
The Red Pony, John Steinbeck
Danny, Champion of the World, Roald Dahl

U

The View From Saturday, E. L. Konigsburg
The Long Winter, Laura I. Wilder
Julie of the Wolves, Jean C. George
Tuck Everlasting, Natalie Babbitt

V

Harry Potter (series), J. K. Rowling
Maniac McGee, Jerry Spinelli
Anne of Green Gables, L. M. Montgomery
Mrs. Frisby and the Rats of NIHM, Robert C. O'Brien

W

I Am a Star: Child of the Holocaust, Inge Auerbacher
The Phantom Tollbooth, Norton Juster
Stowaway, Karen Hesse
After the Dancing Days, Margaret I. Rostkowski

XYZ

Where the Red Fern Grows, Wilson Rawls
Memories of Anne Frank, Alison L. Gold
Carry On, Mr. Bowditch, Jean Lee Latham
Sacajawea, Joseph Bruchac
White Fang, Jack London
A Day No Pigs Would Die, Sylvia Peck
The Hobbit, J. R. R. Tolkien

NONFICTION, INFORMATION BOOKS

Winter Woollies, Tracey Elliott-Reep
Watching the Whales, Graham Meadows
The Red Tailed Hawk, Lola Schaefer
Blackbear Cubs, Alan Lind
Handtools, Helen Depree
Digging Dinosaurs, Judy Nayer
Creepy Creatures, Weldon Owen
Animal Champions, Teri C. Jones
Dinosaur Bones, Marie Gibson
Extreme Sport, Sharon Capobianco
Secrets of the Rainforest, Edward Myers
Chasing Tornadoes, Becky Gold
Living in Space, Judy Nayer
Book of Black Heroes from A–Z, Wade Hudson
Fish Faces, Norbert Wu
Lincoln: A Photobiography, Russell Freedman
Sharks, Dorothy Francis
Eli: A Black Bear, Bonnie H. Taylor
Kooski: A Gray Wolf, Bonnie H. Taylor
Standing Tall: The Stories of Ten Hispanic Americans,
    Argentina Palacios

SERIES BOOKS

School Friends, Bernice Chardiet
The Boxcar Children, Gertrude C. Warner
The Baby-Sitters' Club, Ann M. Martin
Encyclopedia Brown, Donald Sobol
Sideways Stories From Wayside School, Louis Sachar
National Geographic Reading Expeditions
The Great Brain Books, John D. Fitzgerald
Dunc and Amos, Gary Paulsen

AWARD WINNERS

The Whipping Boy, Sid Fleischman
Dogsong, Gary Paulsen
Call It Courage, Armstrong Sperry
The Summer of the Swans, Betsy Byars
My Side of the Mountain, Jean C. George
Caddie Woodlawn, Carol R. Brink
Johnny Tremain, Esther Forbes
Rabbit Hill, Robert Lawson
The Witch of Blackbird Pond, Elizabeth G. Speare
A Wrinkle in Time, Madelene L'Engle
Shadow of a Bull, Maia Wojciechowski
Up a Road Slowly, Irene Hunt
The Slave Dancer, Paula Fox
Bridge to Terabithia, Katherine Paterson
Dicey's Song, Cynthia Voight

Dear Mr. Henshaw, Beverly Clearly
Sarah, Plain & Tall, Patricia MacLachlan
Holes, Louis Sachar
A Year Down Yonder, Richard Peck
The Giver, Lois Lowry
The High King, Lloyd Alexander

MAGAZINES

Girl's Life
Boy's Life
Scholastic Magazine
Nick Jr.
Sports Illustrated for Kids

HOW-TO BOOKS

The Book of Lists for Kids, Sandra Choron
The New Way Things Work, David Macaulay
The Way Things Work Kit, David Macaulay
Scientific American's How Things Work Today,
    Michael Wright and M. N. Patel

CATALOGS

Sports equipment
Toys
Clothing

READERS' THEATER SCRIPTS

http://home.earthlink.net/~hjerman/theatlink.html
http://www.storycart.com/
http://www.aaronshep.com/rt/

DICTIONARIES

Macmillan Dictionary for Students, William D. Halsey

ATLASES

National Geographic Atlas for Young Explorers
Rand McNally Children's Atlas of the United States

THESAURUSES

The Thesaurus for Kids, Evelyn Pesiri
Simon and Schuster Thesaurus for Children,
    Jonathan P. Latimer

CD-ROM ENCYCLOPEDIAS

Encarta
Encyclopedia Britannica
Guinness Book of the Century, David Gould

ENCYCLOPEDIAS

Science Encyclopedia, Dempsey Parr Publishers
World History Encyclopedia, Dempsey Parr Publishers

Use the Collection for Responses to Reading

The well-planned classroom library not only houses materials for reading—it also includes opportunities for responding to reading. We think of it as a repository for providing and explaining a variety of response options, including writing, drawing, and dramatizing: a special place in the classroom that offers students choices of how to express their responses to a book.

Having said this, we also want to point out that the size of your overall classroom and library space will determine how much of the actual responding activity can occur *within* the classroom library itself. (See the next section for more on how to best organize the space allotted to your library.) To maintain an atmosphere conducive to reading, there may be times when you'll need to have your students do their producing and creating in another location. In any case, the library should be seen as the central spot in the room for reader-response idea generation and for the coordination and storage of the supplies that will enable those responses.

First, let's take a look at the supplies you'll need. At right is a list of suggested minimal supplies—writing materials, art supplies, and other kinds of hands-on materials—for an effective classroom library to support reader response.

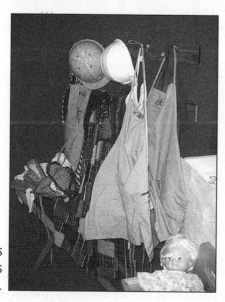

A set of simple costumes and props makes dramatizations more fun.

Recommended (Minimal) Supplies for an Effective Classroom Library

- Recipe cards
- Assorted forms
- Stationery
- Cardboard boxes
- Note cards
- File folders
- Pens, pencils, and markers
- Post-its
- Message pads
- Post office supplies
- Envelopes of various sizes
- Address labels
- Racks for filing papers
- Paper of assorted sizes
- Index cards
- Clipboards
- Stickers
- Greeting cards
- Stamps
- Stamp pads
- Tote bag for mail
- Business forms
- Cardboard and posterboard
- Glue, string, paper clips, stapler
- Puppets
- Fabric
- Simple costumes and props
- Tape recorder

To allow this aspect of your classroom library to be truly successful, you need to make students aware of the great variety of possible responses. You might create a poster display for a Reading Response Menu, such as the one shown below, to help students think about and select an appropriate method for sharing their response to a book or text.

READING RESPONSE MENU

Drawing or Illustrating
Draw a map based on the story's location.
Draw a "Wanted" poster for a character in the story.
Make the story into a comic book or comic strip.
Design a book jacket for the story or book.
Make a comparison chart of several of an author's works.
Make an illustrated time line or story map.
Design a bookmark to market the book to others.

Constructing
Make a character puppet.
Build a model of a favorite part of a story.
Construct a mobile of the story characters.
Construct a game of Trivial Pursuit or Password.
Make a Big Book of the story.
Design character masks for a dramatization.

Writing
Write a poem or song about the story.
Write a letter to a friend about the story.
Write a letter to the author or publisher offering comments.
Rewrite the book or story as a play, radio play, or TV commercial.
Write a new ending to the book or story.
Write an advertisement for the book or story.
Write an imaginary letter to one of the characters.

Dramatizing
Act out the story using costumes and props.
Perform the story as a Readers' Theater dialogue.
Perform the story as a puppet play.
Videotape a TV commercial for the story.
Play charades involving the characters or parts of the story.
Videotape a news interview with one of the characters.

Now that you're familiar with the rationale behind a classroom library and the purposes, functions, and planning that characterize it, your next question may well be: What does an effective classroom library look like? We have several ideas about that. First, one humorous view about how to organize a classroom library.

And now for a more serious take on this important subject.

What an Effective Classroom Library Looks Like: Organization and Layout

Organize to Help Accomplish Your Major Goals

Above all, the space in a classroom library must be organized to encourage comfortable student interactions with books and all other literacy tools or props stored or displayed here. This means that teachers must organize the classroom library with user-friendliness

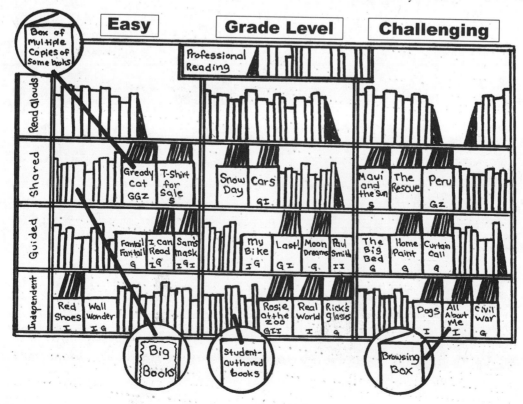

in mind. Displays need to invite students to touch, take, examine, read, write, and talk. Directions posted in the classroom library need to help students figure out what to do, how to do it, where to do it, and when to do it. To do less is to invite mayhem.

The classroom library also needs to be organized so students suffer neither from "browser overload" nor from an inability to reasonably maintain the order and appearance of the area. This means the library should be organized to provide cues for appropriate levels and different types of materials.

You will reap many benefits from carefully organizing the physical space. Doing so can help your students in all the major interactions that you would like to see occur in the classroom library. You may get some good ideas from the three photos below. Each has strengths, which we've highlighted in the captions.

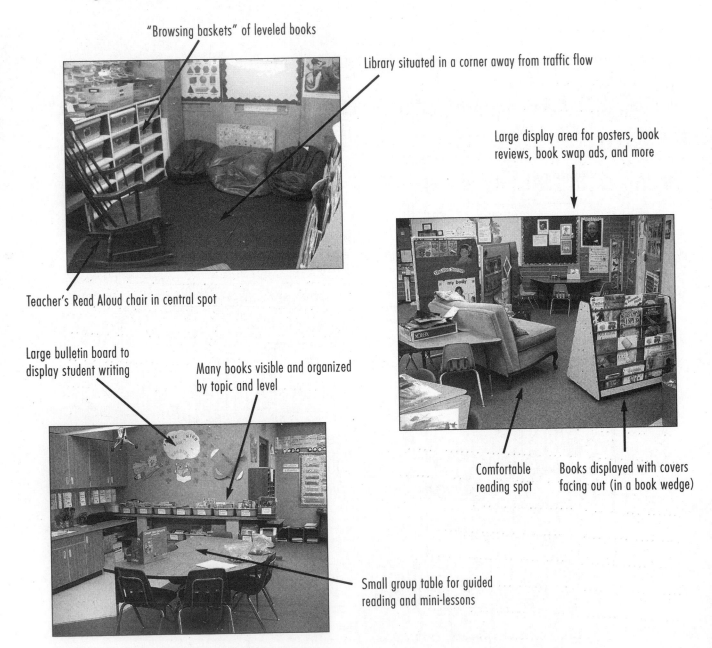

"Browsing baskets" of leveled books

Library situated in a corner away from traffic flow

Large display area for posters, book reviews, book swap ads, and more

Teacher's Read Aloud chair in central spot

Large bulletin board to display student writing

Many books visible and organized by topic and level

Comfortable reading spot

Books displayed with covers facing out (in a book wedge)

Small group table for guided reading and mini-lessons

Other Criteria and Practices for Organizing the Classroom Library

Here are additional criteria and recommended practices for creating and organizing an effective classroom library:

❀ Allocate a space of at least 10 feet by 8 feet within the classroom for the library; this may seem excessive to teachers in overcrowded classrooms, but given the multiple functions served by the library, such an allocation of space is the minimum.

❀ Situate it away from the central, somewhat noisier activities and traffic flow of the classroom.

❀ House smaller book collections or "branches" of the classroom library in learning centers located in more active areas of the classroom.

❀ Provision the classroom library with a large variety of reading materials.

❀ Plan the space for the library so that students are shielded from visual distractions but so that you can view the area from nearly every location in the classroom.

❀ Display materials in the library to pique students' curiosity, invite their contributions, and register their responses. Be intuitive! Here's an example of a "Book Opening" invitation:

COME ONE! COME ALL!

Join me for a Book Opening for the novel
Harry Potter and the Prisoner of Azkaban

AT: 2:00 p.m.
IN: the Classroom Library
ON: Thursday

Come prepared! Bring your favorite prop! Wear a hat (or hood or mask…)! If you've read the book, come ready to talk about your favorite scene. If not, come ready to hear why you should read the book! And we promise not to give away the ending!

COME ONE! COME ALL!

❀ Arrange the books and other media so that they are enticing and easily accessed.

❀ Arrange shelves so that they meet the needs of instruction and students' interests as well as the limitations of children's physical size.

❀ Organize displays around themes and place them in a revolving wire rack.

Displays that show materials clearly and that are well organized will help students find the right books.

❊ Set aside materials and display a menu of options for reacting to and responding to reading materials.

❊ Label shelves to help students keep books and display materials orderly. For younger children you can make labels that include a picture or a computer-generated icon along with words to assist the task of labeling (see the chart, right) and direction posters that contain "rebus" reading. (Rebus reading is language containing intermittent pictures in place of words; it is intended to lower the threshold of reading ability and make the reading of directions easier.)

❊ Put multiple copies of a single title together in a single label to help maintain order and ease of selection. Big Books can be displayed and stored in a number of ways to be discussed in Chapter 4. Sort student books for independent reading by level into "browsing boxes" or "browsing baskets" (as illustrated in the photo at right) to ease the process of book selection and assure an appropriate match of student level with text demands.

Books for independent reading are sorted by level into "browsing baskets."

❉ Label literacy tools or props to help students return them to their proper storage spots. For younger children, picture icons of literacy tools, such as pencils, markers, crayons, paper, and staplers, can be produced along with the word labels to show where materials should be placed after use.

Even the most well-planned classroom library will not run smoothly unless you also set up a system for cleanup and maintenance of the materials stored and displayed in the library. One way you can make the task easier for students is to thoroughly explain the rules ahead of time in a mini-lesson (see Chapter 2 for a sample lesson). You can then post a list, like the following, in a prominent place:

Keeping Our Classroom Library Orderly and Neat

Put books back on the shelf where they belong.

Rearrange chairs and tables so they look the same as when you found them.

Rewind read-along tapes and return them to their cases.

Turn off the tape player.

Return Big Books to their places.

Put display books back in their places.

Check books in or out with the classroom librarian.

Close any computer programs in use.

Turn the computer off if you're the last group of the day.

We want to stress that effective classroom libraries are not the product of accident or evolutionary forces, but rather the result of careful, thoughtful reflection, planning, and organization. Understanding this has helped us and many teachers with whom we've worked take a fresh look at designing functional and effective classroom libraries as the central hub of classroom reading and writing instruction.

Once the classroom library is designed, outfitted with adequate supplies, and ready for students, the *real* work begins. Setting up a library is only the beginning—making optimal use of this resource is integrally tied to careful instructional planning, effective classroom management, and systematic teaching of book selection strategies. In the next chapter, we share research findings about understanding students' book selection behaviors and show you how to teach children effective strategies for selecting books.

CHAPTER 2

Helping Children Make Successful Book Selections

SELECTION/REJECTION

I handled one book

But she said it had

Too lengthy sentences,

Too deep a content,

Too high a vocab level,

Too far up

On the fifth-grade shelf

For a third-grader to understand.

I touched another book

But she said it had

Too short sentences,

Too shallow a content,

Too low a vocab level,

Too far down

On the first-grade shelf

For a third-grader to enjoy.

I chose no more books

They caused

Too much trouble,

Too often

For this third-grader to read.

— Lynette Tandy, Fort Worth, Texas

When children enter a library setting, they often experience something called "browser overload" (Baker, 1986). This means that the sheer number of materials in the library can present students with a sense of being overcome, as well as feeling like a stranger in a strange land. To help children develop a sense of comfort within the library, and to empower them with the ability to choose books well, it is essential that the classroom teacher understand how they go about choosing books. You should know how students become discriminating readers. You should be aware of what actually happens as students figure out what a book has to offer and how they gauge whether a book will fit in with their reading abilities and interests.

The success of a quality, comprehensive reading program depends largely upon the knowledge and competence of the teacher (Darling-Hammond, 1997). Every classroom includes children with a broad range of backgrounds and literacy experiences: Some have had extensive experience with parents, siblings, and others who have modeled the reading process; others have had access to a wide variety of books and other reading materials; and still others have had little or no opportunity to experience the reading process or to handle books or other printed materials.

With this in mind, strive to make a rich array of reading materials available to all children and to properly match materials to each child's needs. And in order to appropriately match books to a student's needs, try to stay aware of the following interrelated sets of understandings, each of which is essential to effective teaching (Fountas and Pinnell, 1999):

- Knowing students' reading processes
- Knowing the levels and challenges found in texts
- Knowing the reading process and how children develop as readers

We add to this list that a teacher must know children's habits, interests, and book selection behaviors and strategies.

In the first half of this chapter, we discuss what children do when selecting books. We also discuss the factors that influence children's selection of books, and how classroom libraries can be designed and arranged to influence and inform their book selection strategies. In the second half of the chapter, we present a series of mini-lessons to show how you can model effective strategies and instruct students on selecting appropriate books for independent reading.

What Children Do When Selecting Books

First-, third-, and fifth-grade children of above-average, average, and below-average reading abilities were observed in a recent study as they selected books (Reutzel and Gali, 1998). The observations were made during the students' weekly visits to check out books in school media centers/libraries. The study's findings focused on how children located books in the school library; how they sampled books in the school library; which factors limited their selection of books during the library period;

and the reasons they gave for choosing or rejecting a book. In addition, the researchers determined the book selection strategies and processes employed by each child observed. The study resulted in a set of generalizations about how students select books and looked at differences that indicated more or less sophisticated approaches. We sum up these generalizations below.

Students typically approach book selection by either entering a predetermined location within the library or simply beginning to browse wherever they are physically in the library. They examine book titles whether they are shelved spine out or cover out. In the case of looking for books shelved spine out, students typically tilt their heads, touch the spines with their fingertips (pointing to titles) and read the title printed along the spine. Next, after pulling the book from its shelf or display position, students often examine the cover. It appears that handling a book is an important part of selection. Once in hand, students open the book and engage in one of four typical sampling behaviors: 1) flip through the pages; 2) read selected text segments; 3) look at the illustrations or diagrams; and/or 4) look at selected pages within the book. After doing these things, students make a judgment about whether they want to keep or reject the book.

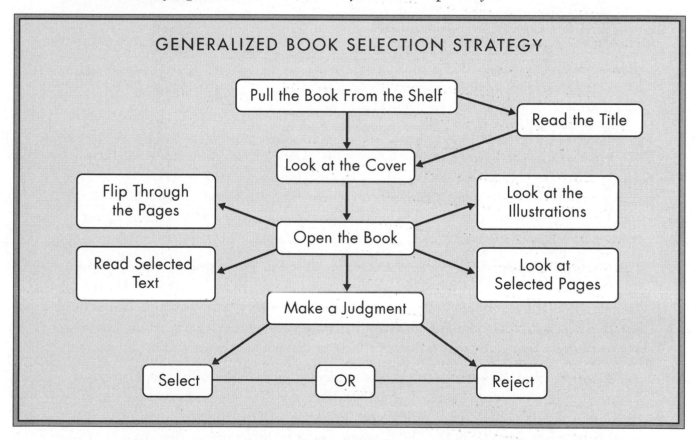

GENERALIZED BOOK SELECTION STRATEGY

Pull the Book From the Shelf → Read the Title → Look at the Cover → Open the Book →

- Flip Through the Pages
- Read Selected Text
- Look at the Illustrations
- Look at Selected Pages

Open the Book → Make a Judgment → Select OR Reject

Although many children follow this generalized set of routine behaviors in selecting books, there were a few children observed in the study who exhibited "outlier" or unique book selection behaviors. One child relied on predetermined specific physical characteristics, such as large print, a limited number of pages, and lots of pictures; for this child, the topic was not as important as size and typographical considerations. Another child, Howie, in fifth grade, had an interesting twist on book selection. After following the general routine of selecting a book, Howie would stack several of them on a table in the library until he had a pile of about six to seven books from which to select. Then, near the end of the library period, he would sit down with his stack and turn them right-side up and spines out to consider them for selection. Next, he would go through each book in somewhat greater depth by skimming a few pages in each. Finally, he would choose two of the six or seven for checkout. Howie's book selection strategy was one of the most sophisticated for dealing with browser overload observed among the children studied.

Four Book Selection Strategies

Based on their 1998 study and other research, Reutzel and Gali (1996, 1998) borrowed from shopping behavior terminology to create several categories of children's book selection strategies. They came up with the following major "book shopping" types:

The **Binge Buyers** are those students who are easily influenced by displays. They tend to select those books in the library that are displayed cover out rather than spine out. These students tend to spend little or no time browsing in the library but rather impulsively grab any book on display to check out.

> ### Students' Book Shopping Behaviors
>
> ❋ Binge Buyers
>
> ❋ Discerning Customers
>
> ❋ Social Shoppers
>
> ❋ Convergent Customers
>
> ❋ Shop Till You Drop Shoppers

The **Discerning Customers** are the informed students. These are the ones who know which books are popular with others. They know of best-selling books, books recommended by the teacher, and books on public library or school reading lists. They comparison-browse for recommended books and then choose from among them after reading selectively from each.

The **Social Shoppers** make book selection a social event. These students travel through the library in a small group. Books are pulled from the shelves and discussed. The Social Shopper students ask others in the group whether or not they have read a particular book and frequently discuss among themselves the contents and other aspects of the book. These students appear heavily influenced by peer comments when selecting a book.

The **Convergent Customers** come to the library with a specific book or topic in mind. These students very often know which books they want to read. They may have heard them read aloud by the teacher or librarian, or they may have other topics in mind. They go directly to the location in the library where books on this topic are displayed or shelved, and will remain there until they've made a selection, whereupon they immediately settle into reading.

Finally, there is the **Shop Till You Drop** crowd. These students often select books in peer groups but may also browse alone. They will spend the entire time allotted for book selection browsing. They typically do not select a book until it becomes apparent that time is running out, and then they will make an impulsive choice for checkout. These students are very often dissatisfied with their choice at a later time and want to take it back and exchange it for another book. Time allowed for browsing seems to be poorly used.

There are a number of discernible reasons for these different styles. Below we take a look at some of the factors that lie behind the choices.

Factors That Influence Book Selection

 Although children have been self-selecting books for many years in classrooms, school libraries, and public libraries, up until 1990 few studies were conducted to learn how, why, when, where, or what influences children's book selections. One of the earliest studies on children's book-selecting behaviors found four major factors: genre, writing style, type size, and illustrations (King, 1967). But this was one of the very few sources of information, and to make matters worse, little research was conducted to investigate how children were trained to select books (Hiebert, Mervar, and Person, 1990; Hancock and Hill, 1988; Baker, 1986).

Some things have been clear for a while. For instance, gender differences have been consistently uncovered over the past few decades (Fischer, 1988; Donovan, Smolkin, and Lomax, 2000). And it's also been found that peer recommendations often outweigh teacher recommendations among intermediate-grade students (Wendelin and Zinck, 1983). Given the nature of these kinds of influences and factors, it is probably not surprising that a continuing misfit between children's book selections and their individual reading levels has been reaffirmed (Reutzel and Gali, 1998; Donovan, Smolkin, and Lomax, 2000).

In one study by Kay Mervar (1989), second-grade students were given a pre-selected set of five books and asked to choose one and state their reasons for doing so. Observations of children's book selection *behaviors* under these circumstances yielded no differences between children experiencing literature-based reading instruction and those receiving reading instruction in a more traditional, basal reader program. But there was one notable difference: When students were asked to explain *why* they chose a book, those in literature-based classrooms were able to offer more elaborate responses than those in traditional reading programs.

In another study (Timion, 1992), a second-grade teacher investigated children's book selection strategies in a year-long research project. She instituted a reading program in which primarily trade books rather than basal readers were used as the instruction texts. When the basal reader was used, it was used like an anthology, with basal stories selected here and there rather than in a linear fashion, from front to back, as would be typical. She also read aloud daily. When she was unable to read an entire book aloud, she offered a book talk (see the mini-lesson at the end of this chapter for more about book talks) to pique student interest. As the year progressed, she began to hold individual conferences with students to assess their increasing reading abilities as well as to study their interests and reading habits. She also increased daily reading of related texts selected from the classroom library. Students read both in pairs and independently on a daily basis. As children made greater and greater use of the books in the classroom library, Timion (1992) remarked, "Students were reading and replacing books from our classroom library every day, and as fall turned into winter, organizing all the books in the classroom library was becoming a real problem."

After the winter break, a reading incentive program was added to the classroom routine, and a parent questionnaire asking why children selected particular books was sent out. Answers from parents' observations in January revealed that second-grade children selected books for four major reasons: 1) the books had been read before; 2) the books were in a home library; 3) the author was a favorite; and 4) the book was in the classroom library. By April of the same year, Timion (1992) noted that children's reasons for selecting books had expanded to roughly ten. These reasons reflected greater sophistication as the students' skills and abilities increased. By the end of the school year, the most common reason given for selecting a book was "I can read [it]."

Reutzel and Gali's (1998) study of children's book selection strategies revealed the most extensive information related to factors that influence choices. Motivations for choosing a book among first-, third-, and fifth-grade students of above-average, average, and below-average reading abilities included the factors, in priority order, listed in the box at right.

The top three priorities on this list—personal valuing, physical characteristics, and topic/theme connections—influenced 76 percent of the students' book selections.

> **Motivations for Choosing a Book (First-, Third-, and Fifth-Graders)**
>
> ❖ Perceived personal value
>
> ❖ Physical characteristics of the book
>
> ❖ Topic or theme: connections among books
>
> ❖ Genre preference
>
> ❖ Author preference
>
> ❖ Personal recommendations
>
> ❖ Character knowledge
>
> ❖ Displayed books and books read aloud by teachers

Personal Valuing

Students most often chose personal valuing as a criterion for selecting a book, using statements such as, "This looks like a good book." Or a student might say, "I think this book will be fun to read." Students frequently chose a book based upon a first-blush perceived value. In fact, the perceived value typically reflected the student's purpose for reading the book. If the student was approaching reading from an "aesthetic" stance, a desire for an emotional or recreational experience in reading (Rosenblatt, 1978), then she usually expressed anticipation of the personal experience to be gained from reading selected fiction and narratives. If, on the other hand, a student was approaching reading from an "efferent" stance, or a desire to learn and gain information (Rosenblatt, 1978), then she mentioned an overarching topic or theme and selected expository and nonfiction books.

Physical Characteristics

Physical characteristics of books also played a role in children's book selection. Children seemed to be very aware of the length and difficulty of each book as judged by the number of pages, the number of pictures, and the size of the type. For some children, there seemed to be a social prestige attached to selecting "fat" books with few pictures and small type fonts. Other children were comfortable choosing books that were easy, using the opposite criteria—a "thin" book with many pictures and a larger type font.

Topics or Themes

Students' book selections were influenced by topics or themes currently taught in the classroom. For example, if electromagnetism was being studied in science class, then books on this topic were often selected. Or, if the American Revolution was the topic of discussion in the classroom, then children chose fictional or nonfictional accounts about this event.

Students often spoke of having read "other books like this" as a reason for selecting a book. Sometimes this meant that they had read books of a similar genre—for instance, other biographies, fairy tales, and so on. Sometimes this meant that they had read books on a similar topic. But it was clear that making "intertextual links," as described by Hartman (1995), was a guiding principle in book selection among children.

Genre and Author Preference

Genre was also a clear influence on students' book selection behaviors. Students remarked that they liked to read autobiographies, journal accounts, and fictional accounts, but the series genre—books such as the Magic Tree House (Osborne) series; the Bailey Schools Kids books (Dadey and Jones); and the Secrets of Droon series (Abbott)—seemed to have the most appeal. This influence upon children's book selection appeared to be motivated by the set of books and by knowledge of the author and the character(s) within a series. Common statements were, "I like R. L. Stein's Goosebump books" or "My favorite books are the Baby-Sitters' Club books." Series books were quite popular among intermediate-grade boys and girls alike.

Sharing, discussing, and getting recommendations about a book are important aids in book selection for some students.

Personal Recommendations

Personal recommendations about a book or book series from other children, a librarian, parents, and the teacher were also motivation for selecting a book. This was particularly true among those children who approached book selection as "social shoppers," requiring peer input and approval prior to selection. Sharing, discussing, and getting recommendations was clearly important to many young children in selecting a book for independent reading or for learning about a specific topic.

Character Knowledge

Some students talked of searching for and selecting books based on favorite characters. Among younger children, Curious George was a popular choice. Older children expressed an attachment to the character of Harry Potter and wanted to find and check out books based on him. The personal knowledge of a character in a book often motivated the selection of other books containing that character.

Displays and Read-Alouds

Displaying books increased their likelihood of selection. Students often inspected "books lying around" in the library, on the librarian's desk, and on tables, with the covers clearly visible. In fact, these books were twice as likely to get picked up and inspected—from the "flip test" to a partial read. Clearly, much like showcased goods at retail outlets, displayed books attracted students' attention far more often than those shelved with only the spine showing.

Showcased books, especially those displayed with covers facing out, will attract student attention.

Along with displaying certain books, a teacher or librarian provided a strong influence on children's selections by reading a book aloud. The teacher or librarian not only read aloud, but also frequently explained or extolled the quality, content, and style of an author's work. In many ways, these individuals "blessed the books" for selection (Gambrell, 2001).

It is especially heartening to note that a teacher can be so influential when we realize the arbitrary or even quixotic nature of some of the other factors listed above. There is an additional reason to make the teacher's role key—the guidance he or she can provide to below-average readers.

Below-average readers most often chose books that were ill-fitted to their reading levels. Because below-average readers were usually boys, the books selected were generally nonfiction information texts containing a heavy conceptual load. Both in purpose and supposed prestige, below-average readers seemed to approach book selection with a pragmatic orientation—the purpose of which was to get information and learn, not to enjoy.

Unsurprisingly, above-average readers seemed to select books more appropriate to their reading levels (Donovan, Smolkin, and Lomax, 2000). Their purposes for reading often guided whether they would choose an easy or difficult book, a fiction or nonfiction book. If the book was for enjoyment, they would usually choose a familiar, easy narrative text. If it was for learning, they would choose unfamiliar, difficult information texts. In short, above-average readers tended to be far more strategic in the books they selected.

In the next section, we'll see how the way in which a teacher sets up and arranges the classroom library can help guide and influence *all* readers to make better, more appropriate book selections.

How to Arrange Your Classroom Library to Guide and Influence Children's Book Selection

Understanding students' book selection behaviors and the environmental conditions that influence them naturally leads to several conclusions about how a classroom library can be arranged to best guide and inform children in their choices. From the physical layout to the furnishings and displays, how the classroom library is set up will either serve to assist or inhibit students as they go about the task of selecting a book for independent reading.

Label Shelves

Labeling shelves clearly is very helpful. It is a good idea to provide labels that point out where different genres of reading materials are located. For students seeking nonfiction books or books on specific topics, it's helpful to label shelves or other locations by noting the topic or theme of the books. Examples of label categories to consider placing around the classroom library are shown below.

Examples of Labels, by Category, for Classroom Library Shelves

Reading Levels: [Easy] [Grade Level] [Challenging]

General Topics: [Science] [History] [Geography] [Health]

Genres: [Fairy Tales] [Folk Tales] [Biographies] [Plays] [Poetry] [Comics]

Themes: [Insects] [Rocks] [Ghost Stories] [Explorers] [U.S. Civil War]

Best Books: [Most Selected] [Class Favorites] [Teacher-Recommended]

Post Directions

To provide children with a holistic understanding of the classroom library organization and layout, a map can be produced and displayed near the entrance to the library.

    If there are specific limitations placed on the use of the classroom library or of certain resources, a reminder chart like the one shown below can help students to remember boundaries and expectations. Such a display can also tell children where they can go to get help in finding books, selecting books, and checking out books from the classroom library.

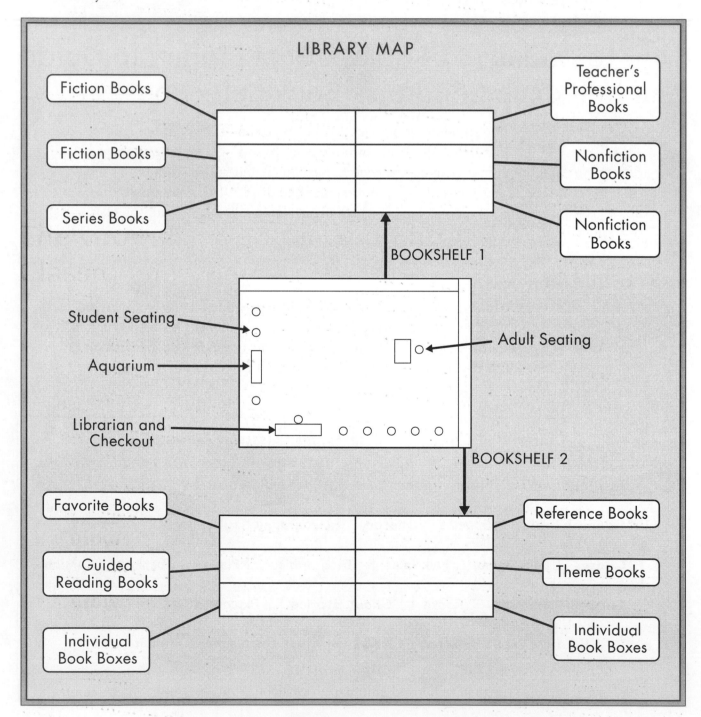

LIBRARY MAP

Fiction Books

Fiction Books

Series Books

Teacher's Professional Books

Nonfiction Books

Nonfiction Books

BOOKSHELF 1

Student Seating

Aquarium

Adult Seating

Librarian and Checkout

BOOKSHELF 2

Favorite Books

Guided Reading Books

Individual Book Boxes

Reference Books

Theme Books

Individual Book Boxes

Classroom Library Rules Poster

Two books at most may be checked out at a time.

Books are due back within a week.

Books from Browsing Boxes may only go home overnight.

Return checked-out books first thing in the morning.

Do not disturb someone who is quietly reading.

Please whisper in the classroom library.

If you need help, first ask a friend or consult the library map.

If you still need help, ask the student librarian.

After trying these steps, ask the teacher or other adult helper.

Display Books With Covers Facing Out

From the studies cited earlier, it is clear that the way in which books are displayed can play a significant role in assisting students in making selections. Books displayed with the covers out were much more likely to be examined and selected than shelved books. There are many ways to display books. Some teachers have found that when local retail stores go out of business, there are often greeting-card display shelving and rotating wire racks that can be had free or at a minimum cost. This idea and others are listed below. Remember—surrounding children with displays produces an environment where books are always present and where book selection becomes a natural activity.

Rotating wire racks, which can often be found at little or no cost, provide accessible book displays.

Ideas for Displaying Books

❖ On rotating wire racks

❖ On tabletops and bookshelf tops

❖ On windowsills

❖ In book baskets in different spots around the room

❖ In vinyl rain gutters affixed below bulletin boards, along windowsills, and across bookshelves

Use Posters and Whiteboards

You can set up other displays in the classroom library to help students select appropriate books. You might, for instance, post a summary such as the one shown below of the main reasons students make the book choices they do. This may help them remember all of the possibilities.

Or students can make posters to advertise their favorite books. A display of "kid" book reviews and recommendations on a dry-erase board can guide students' book selections. Children not only enjoy reading the reviews and recommendations but also enjoy placing their own ideas on this display. We have found that the chance to contribute to the display motivates children to read books. Children's choices and other best-seller lists (see Chapter 1, page 14) may be displayed on posters; laminating these posters and using a water-based marker makes erasing and updating quick and easy. You might also use posters that contain lists of the top ten books recommended in the Teacher's Choice list published annually in *The Reading Teacher* (International Reading Association).

How Do Readers Choose Books?

By skimming the book—what is the book about?

By the illustrations

By the cover

By a favorite author

By a favorite character (or series)

By a favorite or interesting topic

By reading the front flap or blurb

Because it's a favorite or familiar book

Because it's a "just right" book

— Diane Miness, first-grade teacher, Dutch Neck School, Princeton Junction, NJ

Use Chart Pads for Showing Connections Among Books

One effective way to bolster children's emerging sense of connections among books with similar structure or content is to involve the class in creating an intertextual graphic organizer display. This kind of display not only informs children of other similar books but also encourages them to include their own contributions. Start by setting up a large chart tablet. Be sure to leave the first page or two of the chart pad blank for a table of contents (which will take shape as the graphic organizers are created). Give each separate graphic organizer its own page within the chart pad collection. You can complete the first few organizers with the whole class. After that, students can use the chart tablet to look up books that have been included in the collection; fill in missing information on a particular organizer on their own; or eventually insert a graphic organizer for a set of books themselves. All the books used for this activity should be available in the classroom library.

An example of an intertextual graphic organizer that requires student input to complete is shown below.

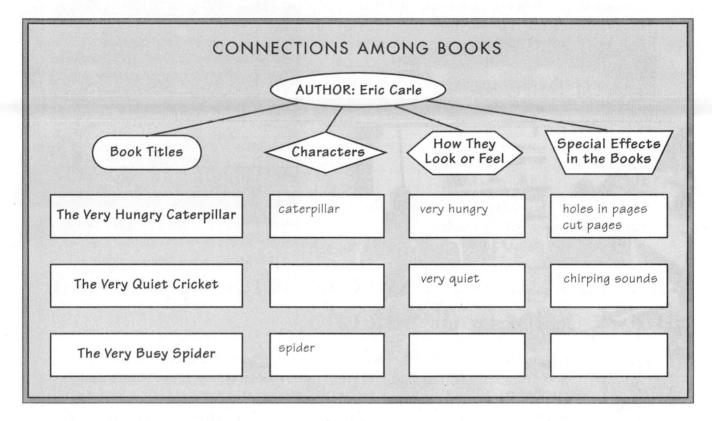

CONNECTIONS AMONG BOOKS

AUTHOR: Eric Carle

Book Titles	Characters	How They Look or Feel	Special Effects in the Books
The Very Hungry Caterpillar	caterpillar	very hungry	holes in pages cut pages
The Very Quiet Cricket		very quiet	chirping sounds
The Very Busy Spider	spider		

Organize Books Logically

You can also help to guide students' book selections by grouping the book collection around interests, authors, themes, topics, series, characters, genre, or reading levels. Periodically inviting students to fill out reading and interest surveys can be a step toward understanding and meeting their needs and interests. You'll find an example of a reading interest survey in Chapter 5.

Baskets filled with books by the same author, about the same character, at the same reading level, or on the same topic or theme help students to select books more effectively. Reserving sections of

Baskets filled with books by one author or on a related theme help students to select books.

the shelves for collections of reference materials or books of differing levels helps students to know where to look for books that interest or challenge them.

Set Up Books at Children's Eye Level

In more senses than one, it is important that students select books on their level. Here we mean eye level! As often as possible, shelved and displayed books should be at students' eye levels or below. Books placed above these levels are unlikely to be touched or selected (Reutzel and Gali, 1998). Try to organize book collections of similar purpose or type horizontally rather than vertically. Bookshelves more than a foot above students' eye levels are best for storing books that the teacher intends to reserve for Read Alouds, shared reading, or guided reading.

Shelved and displayed books are best positioned at students' eye level or below.

What You Can Do to Give Children Appropriate Strategies for Book Selection

When children enter the classroom library without preparation or guidance, they are flooded with questions. Where do I look? How do I know what I want? Who can help me if I can't find what I want? How do I know this book is right for me? When I am done reading a book, what should I do then? How do I get ready to read a book? What if the book I want is already checked out? Since Timion's (1992) research has shown that for some, if not many, the hardest part of reading is selecting a book, it seems that students will need teacher guidance and instruction to optimize their book selection and reading strategies.

Below we offer a set of highly motivational book selection activities. Then, after a brief look at the importance of making adaptations to ensure equal access for all students, we provide several book selection and reading strategy lessons to use in helping students to find the right book. The lessons are sequenced to help students develop an overall strategic approach to selecting books. To begin, students need to gain an understanding of the geographical layout of the classroom library. Next, it is important to *talk* about books as a way to acquaint children with the contents of the classroom library. Third, it will be helpful if you model strategies for locating, sampling, and selecting a book. Finally, after finding a book, students need to learn how to determine whether or not the book they chose is appropriately matched to their own reading level and ability.

MOTIVATIONAL BOOK SELECTION ACTIVITIES

1. **Book Check Out:** A check-out system for classroom library books can also serve as a real motivator. On the inside back cover of library books, tape a three- by five-inch index card horizontally, to be used as a pocket. Place another index card vertically inside the pocket; this one is for students to use as they check out a book. Students should remove and sign the card and place it in a simple recipe box you make available. This system results in an ongoing record of which students in which year have read a particular book. Most children are very interested in finding out who has read a book previously. If they discover that a sibling, friend, or acquaintance has signed the card, chances are great that they will be really motivated to read the book.*

2. **Book Reviews:** After children read a book in the classroom library that they really love, they can opt to get a form called "Book Review," which enables them to write a letter to a future reader. (See the book review below for one example.) They can use the review to give tips for understanding the story or reasons to read it, or to describe responses or feelings they experienced. The book review is folded and put into the book. It protrudes from the top of the book enough to catch future readers' eyes and entice them to read it. If nothing else, other students will read the reviews! Students usually love this system, and it encourages reading.*

3. **Recommended Reads:** Students don't always have to do a full review. Instead, they might do a "recommended read" Post-it. When they have finished reading a book from the classroom library that they would like to recommend, tell them to get a Post-it from a basket in the library and write down the book's title and author, along with their own name. They should then stick the Post-it in the appropriate genre spot on a recommended reading post (a simple stand-up post made out of posterboard and divided into genres). Students should be encouraged to scan the post frequently; they can pick up ideas easily about what to read this way.*

4. **Put Yourself in Another Reader's Shoes:** Pair up your students and tell them that today they are going to become mind readers. For five minutes, they are to converse together about the kinds of books they love to read and their interests in general. Then have them go to the shelves and pick a book they think their partners would love, taking into account what their partners have just revealed about their reading tastes and interests. Back at their seats, books in hand, they are to describe to each other what they've selected, and why they

> The Voyage of the Frog By Gary Paulsen
> Report By LIAM
> This book is about a 14 year old David whose uncle died of cancer. His last wishes were for David to take his boat, "The Frog," and scatter his ashes in the Pacific where no land is visible. Then a huge storm hits knocks him unconscious and then he wakes up to find 200 gallons of water in the cabin. If I was in his position I would have given up but instead he gets out a pump and starts pumping water. Then he runs into a huge group of whales then he encounters a whale research ship who gives him supplies before he heads home. I really liked this book because it had drama, sorrow, joy, remorse, and loyalty. I also like it because it is about a boy my age on an epic journey and that is fun to read.

think their partners would love it. Children can then opt to read the books hand-selected and recommended to them, or not.**

---

* Ideas from Jean Turner, fourth-grade teacher, Mt. Loafer Elementary School, Salem, UT
** Idea from Judy Freeman, children's literature consultant, *Book Talk* columnist for *Instructor* magazine, and author of *More Books Kids will Sit Still For* (Bowker/Greenwood, 1995)

Ensuring Equal Access for All Students

Children with special needs require adaptations within the classroom library to ensure they will have equal access to the knowledge, strategies, and materials. Teachers in inclusion classrooms, where children with a variety of disabilities have been mainstreamed into the traditional learning context, need to be aware of and ready to accommodate the special needs of all learners. If a regular classroom teacher is unaware of the accommodations needed, then consultation with the special education faculty within the school is a first step.

For students with hearing impairments, it is often helpful to provide directions and rules in traditional block printing. Letters should be produced without distracting colors in a simple unadorned type style, such as Helvetica sans serif.

If a student knows American Sign Language, then you can post directions, rules, and guidelines using the symbols and icons of ASL. It may be necessary to learn some minimal sign language or to request a trained aide. You may also need to rewrite lesson plans in simple words if a child with hearing impairments has minimal reading abilities.

For students with visual impairments, you may need to provide rules, directions, shelving labels, and a special collection of books printed in a larger font or even Braille. Further, books on CD-ROM or tape can be made available to assist the visually impaired student. In addition, you might appoint a classroom buddy or guide to help the student make appropriate selections from available adapted materials in the classroom library.

For children with mobility issues, teachers should make appropriately leveled books accessible by removing obstacles around or in front of shelving. You can place browsing books in plastic baskets on lower shelves or on tables to help make books accessible. Students who cannot physically hold or manipulate books can use special headgear to operate the keys or the special "touch screen" of a computer. Books for these students will need to be provided as computer software or via other technological formats.

For students who are learning English as a second language, the teacher should include books in the classroom library printed in the students' first language. Teaching children how to read in their first language and then helping them to transfer this ability to reading and writing in the second language is strongly encouraged by research (Freeman and Freeman, 1992; Fitzgerald, 1995; Goldenberg, 2001).

As part of the structure, design, and planning of the classroom library as well as student lessons on usage, you'll need to make appropriate accommodations and adaptations for ensuring equal access for all students. We recommend that you refer to the discussion above and to other special education sources for specific ideas about what kinds of adaptations may be required.

Getting to Know the Library

Understanding the Context for This Lesson

To avoid browser overload and to facilitate book selection, teachers need to fully explain to children how the classroom library is organized and operated. Students need to be oriented prior to use and periodically during the school year if teachers wish to maintain successful and optimal use of the classroom library.

Sample Mini-Lesson

LESSON: Orienting Students to the Classroom Library

Purpose: To help students successfully, easily, and quickly locate books and other print materials to support their learning and reading development.

Necessary Supplies/Materials: Watercolor-based markers, large posterboard (3), chart paper, different-sized labels, computer and printer for printing labels, pointer, push pins, and tape.

Modeling and Instructing:

Rules, Behaviors, and Limitations

Seat children comfortably within the classroom library space where they can see the shelving and the affixed labels. Talk about what is to be accomplished while in the library. Tasks and purposes may range from browsing for a good book to read to finding a book on a specific topic to aid in writing a science report. Involve the children and encourage their own ideas as you draft rules to make the classroom library an orderly and purposeful place. Explain that, once the draft is complete, you will mount posters within the library of acceptable and unacceptable behaviors for students to refer to as they self-monitor and check their personal behavior. For example, students might ask how many books may be taken from the classroom library at any given time and how long these may be kept. Incorporate this in the rules. Other items may speak to the amount of time a student can use the library each day or the conditions under which a student can use it (e.g., after assigned work or other classroom tasks are completed).

Organization

Prepare a classroom library map (see the map on page 40 for an example) to post on the wall that indicates the location and organization of reading and print materials. Begin by pointing to the map and telling children they can consult it if they forget how the library is organized. With younger children, be sure to use pictures, icons, or rebus reading to accompany the text or labels. Connect the map to the actual furnishings, areas, shelves, and labels by pointing to each as it is discussed.

Having developed rules for use and behavior as well as having shown the children orienting signs and labels, ask hypothetical questions such as, "If I wanted to find a book for my own, independent reading, where would I look?" Or ask, "If I wanted to make sure I could read a book, how can I know where I should look?" Invite a few children to think aloud about how they would answer these and other questions. Be sure to ask them if they have other questions they would like answered, then close the lesson with a quick review of the map and organization.

Monitoring Success: Observe the behaviors of two children daily using the displays on organization, rules, and behaviors until each child in the class has been observed. This should be done to determine each child's understanding and use of the classroom library.

Book Talks

Understanding the Context for This Lesson

A book talk is a time set aside for simply talking about a book that students may or may not have read; it is a way for teachers, parents, and peers to share their feelings, opinions, and recommendations. A book talk is intended to mimic the "dinner time" conversation

Sample Mini-Lesson

LESSON: *Giving a Book Talk on* Harry Potter and the Goblet of Fire

Purpose: To stimulate students' interest in reading this particular book by J. K. Rowling, as well as to engage in reading the series of Harry Potter books.

Necessary Supplies/Materials: One or more copies of the book for sharing, display, and checkout.

Modeling and Instructing: Begin by selecting a book that you have read or with which you are familiar (perhaps through a review or recommendation). Obtain at least one copy of the book for display and for independent reading in your classroom library. If it is a picture book and can be read in a single sitting, you may want to introduce it by reading it aloud to your students. However, if reading the book aloud requires more than a single sitting and it is not one you intend to read from cover to cover but would like students to know about, then a book talk is the right approach to take.

Next, gather the class, a small group, or an individual child for sharing a book talk. Show them the book as the title is read aloud. If possible, tell students something about the author's life, writing style, and interests. After this brief introduction to the book and author, share elements of the plot or story line. One common practice is to tell students something about the book and then read aloud a portion of it where the "problem" of the story line is described, thus leaving students with the question "What will happen next?" In effect, the object of a book talk is to "hook" students on reading the book by giving them just enough to pique their interest. Once this has been accomplished, the book is put

on display for independent reading or checkout.

Here's how a book talk on *Harry Potter and the Goblet of Fire* might go:

1. Show the cover of the book while reading the title aloud.

2. Read the back flap aloud to children, telling them about other books in the Harry Potter series.

3. Tell students about J. K. Rowling's life and how she was destitute and living in poverty when she began writing her first Harry Potter book. Relate her subsequent successes and the fact that these books are so popular they have been translated into multiple languages to be read by children around the world.

4. Introduce the characters and the setting. Tell them about Harry Potter's interesting friends, the Weasleys, and his family, the Dudleys, and about his schooling at Hogwarts and his desire to be just a normal fourteen-year-old. Then set up the book's conflict, leaving them wondering what will happen to Harry, as he is anything but a "normal" fourteen-year-old—even by a "wizard's" standards.

5. Place the book(s) on display in the classroom library so that it is ready for reading or checkout.

Monitoring Success: Observe children and the display shelf during independent reading time. Check to determine if the book has been checked out or has been selected for in-class reading.

about a book someone in the family has read. Your main goal here is to expand students' knowledge of available and interesting books to be read. Holding a book talk is such a valuable practice that it may be used at least daily if not several times each day.

This practice is especially important for children in intermediate grades, as many of the books appropriately read at these grade levels cannot be read aloud in a single sitting like those shared in the early years. As a consequence, intermediate-grade children who have typically achieved some level of reading proficiency and fluency actually know about fewer books to read than they did in their younger years. Teachers who have used this approach on a daily basis have observed two unsurprising but welcome outcomes: 1) book-talk books are often the first selected for checkout; and 2) book talks increase the amount of reading students choose to do in school and out.

A variation on the book talk is called the *book sell*. Any student who is motivated to share a book can come up with a book sell and present it to a small group of students or to the whole class. The steps of the book sell are outlined in this poster,* which you might wish to use as a model for one you create and mount in your own classroom library.

How to Do a Book Sell

Tell the title of the book.

Say who the author of the book is.

Tell a little about the story. Is it funny? Is it sad?
Does it touch your heart? Tell a little about what
happens in the story.

Tell something "special" about the story. Show a favorite
picture or part.

Would you recommend that others read it? Why?

REMEMBER: Anyone can do a Book Sell. It can be done for any
kind of book that you read. Any book that you think is GREAT
would be super to use!

— Diane Miness, first-grade teacher, Dutch Neck School, Princeton Junction, NJ

Finding a Book to Read

Understanding the Context for This Lesson

Finding a book to read isn't always easy for young children. Each child has a different set of interests, purposes, needs, and abilities. Helping children to develop a strategic approach to book selection requires that teachers and librarians think aloud, demonstrate, and reveal how they go about this process.

Sample Mini-Lesson

LESSON: *Selecting a Book in the Classroom Library*

Purpose: To stimulate interest in browsing the book collection and to help students learn a general strategy for selecting a book, including determining a purpose for reading.

Necessary Supplies/Materials: Genre wheel (see page 105), reading interest inventory (see page 104), and a book selection strategy flow chart (see page 33).

Modeling and Instructing: Research reveals there are several considerations that should be carefully weighed as a lesson is prepared for helping students to develop strategic behaviors for selecting books.

First, students need help to determine their purpose for selecting a book. Are they looking for a book to read for enjoyment, what Rosenblatt (1978) has called an aesthetic experience? Or are they looking for a book to read for information, what Rosenblatt has called an efferent purpose? Determining this is important in order to send children to specific locations within the classroom library for browsing.

Second, students need help in narrowing their purposes to a topic or genre. If they are looking for an enjoyable read or story, they should be thinking about the various fiction or narrative genres, such as fictional biographies, mysteries, drama, tall tales, fairy tales, and poetry. If they are looking to gather, sort, organize, or report information, then they should be thinking about connections, curriculum themes, or topics.

If students do not have a particular purpose, browsing will probably be somewhat aimless unless you provide specific instruction in this area. With such instruction, browsing can help students find a book that "catches their fancy" or stimulates an interest.

For these students, a book selection strategy lesson must provide a framework that helps them to reach out to others for recommendations and ideas. These students will benefit from a more social approach toward selecting books. They may want to ask or interview friends, siblings, teachers, parents, or the librarian for recommendations; quickly look at displayed materials; or use a genre wheel to help them find a variety of reading selections. Once the elements of purpose and interest have been addressed, students will need guidance to develop strategies for sampling books from the shelves, narrowing their options, and making an appropriate selection.

Here are the steps of this modeling process:

1. Demonstrate for students, in a think-aloud, how you determine a purpose in selecting a book.

2. Model the use of the genre wheel to stimulate interests.

3. Model the use of the interest inventory to gather recommendations and ideas for book selection.

4. Finally, show and model the generalized book selection strategy shown in the flow chart using at least two different book selection examples.

Monitoring Success: Observe children informally on a daily basis to check the use of these book selection aids. Reinforce the use of these strategies with students.

Sample Mini-Lesson

LESSON: *Selecting a "Just Right" or Appropriately Leveled Book From the Classroom Library*

Purpose: To help students learn the location and system for leveled books in the classroom library, as well as to demonstrate the use of a general strategy for evaluating the appropriate difficulty of a book.

Necessary Supplies/Materials: Different colors of cloth tape on the bindings of books that indicate varying levels of reading difficulty; shelves labeled, as noted earlier, with descriptors indicating general difficulty levels (e.g., easy, grade level, challenging); a poster chart showing the "three fingers" strategy for determining the appropriate level of reading materials.

Modeling and Instructing: In New Zealand schools, books carry a small piece of magenta-colored cloth tape on the binding of the easiest books, both in the classroom library and in the central school collection of guided reading materials. A similar scheme for identifying book levels can be incorporated into the design of classroom libraries. This allows students to know immediately whether or not certain books contain the right mix of known to unknown words to optimize their own reading success.

Another approach is to teach children the three-fingers technique (Allington, 2001) for evaluating the appropriateness of a book's difficulty before selection. This process involves reading one page in a book and placing a finger on each unknown word as the child reads from the page. If the child places more than three fingers on unknown words for each page sampled, then the book is most likely going to be more difficult than is optimal. This is not to suggest a given book should be immediately

dismissed as a choice, but rather to say that if the purpose for reading that book is for enjoyment rather than to obtain information, the student is likely to struggle more than would typically be considered "enjoyable."

Here is a summary of these two aids for helping students make "just right" choices:

1. Show children and remind them of the shelving labels displayed on each bookcase or shelf in the classroom library. Each student should know which level of materials he or she reads most comfortably. (Also, students should understand that everyone began by reading the "early" books and that these are not books to be avoided.) If cloth tape is used, children should know the levels of the marked books as they will be used in their guided reading experiences to indicate the "just right" match that is desirable for optimal reading.

2. Next, using the steps mentioned earlier, demonstrate the three-fingers technique for judging the proportion of known to unknown words in a book to be selected. As a reminder, you can also display a poster in the classroom library that illustrates the steps in the three-fingers technique.

By using the general levels of difficulty indicated by shelf labeling, binder marking, and the three-fingers technique, children should be able to maximize the success of their own book selections.

Monitoring Success: Observe children informally on a daily basis to check the use of these book selection aids. Reinforce the use of these strategies.

Checking the Reading Level

Understanding the Context for This Lesson

Many children select books that are either too difficult or too easy for their reading development. The best situation exists when students are reading books with just the right amount of challenge. Fountas and Pinnell (1999) indicate that "just right" books should contain a proportion of about 90 percent known words to about 10 percent unknown words. The purpose of teaching this lesson is to direct students to the shelves where appropriate leveled materials are stored in the classroom library, as well as to demonstrate for students an easy technique for evaluating the difficulty of a book on their own.

The following two posters may give you some ideas for signs you can mount in your own classroom library. The first one shows a variation of the three-fingers technique; the second is aimed at helping students deliberately choose books with varying reading difficulty levels, depending on their purposes at the time.

How to Choose a "Just Right" Book

※ Choose your book.

※ Open your book to the middle.

※ Start to read.

※ Hold up a finger for each tricky word.

※ If you have to hold up your thumb as well, the book is too challenging…choose another.

> —Diane Miness, first-grade teacher, Dutch Neck School, Princeton Junction, NJ

How to Choose Just the Right Book

※ **JR** Just Right—This book makes sense. I can read most of the words, but I'm not bored. I can improve my mind a bit, but it's not a brain strainer!

※ **DB** Dessert Book—This book is really easy. My predictions match; I can retell the story with details, it's relaxing, and it's a good old book!

※ **CB** Challenge Book—This book has new ideas. It's a little difficult, with two to three new words on each page, and I need to think a lot. I learned a lot but I had to work hard.

> —Diane Miness, first-grade teacher, Dutch Neck School, Princeton Junction, NJ

CHAPTER 3

How Does the Classroom Library Support Reading *to* Children?

It is time for "old favorites" and the first-grade children are gathered on the rug at the front of the room. Ms. Wilson has selected three of her students' favorite books for possible reading today. She tells her students, "Today we are going to read one of your favorite books. I have picked out three books from our classroom library that we have really enjoyed reading." The students are introduced to the three selections available for Read Aloud today. They choose *Tikki, Tikki, Tembo* (Mosel, 1968).

When the Read Aloud is finished, several children demonstrate how well they can recite the very long name that is the centerpiece of the book. José asks Miss Wilson to read the story again. Miss Wilson reminds José that this is a book that is in the classroom library and that when he visits this area during independent reading and writing time, he might wish to have a classmate or volunteer read it to him again.

A teacher, like Ms. Wilson, who has developed and organized a well-functioning classroom library, is in an excellent position to use print and electronic media to support instructional goals and to aid student learning. This kind of classroom provides a real opportunity to do thoughtful Read Alouds. With an established and well-organized classroom library as a resource, you are able to be very purposeful in what you select to read to children. In the subsequent two chapters, we will explore how a classroom library helps children to access relevant material to read with others and on their own. But in this chapter, we will focus on the utility of a classroom library to Read Alouds.

The in-class library provides an ideal resource from which the teacher draws Read Aloud text and through which the student can readily locate books and stories that have been read aloud. In addition to supporting the teacher's Read Aloud efforts, the classroom library provides a home for student-generated stories and a comfortable place for these stories to be read aloud by the author. The classroom library becomes the quarry from which the teachers and the students mine many valuable literacy gems.

Student-created stories are shelved under published books in this classroom library.

Why We Should Read Aloud to Children in the First Place

Many teachers have long understood the value of reading aloud to children. Not only is it a wonderful way to introduce students to the pleasures found in books, it is also clearly the most basic building block in supporting a child's future success with reading. Children who are exposed to Read Alouds from an early age show greater interest in reading as they move forward in life (Campbell, 2001). Hearing high-quality books read aloud by an enthusiastic teacher or a supportive parent is an important factor in motivating children to become independent readers.

There is an additional important benefit. Because a reader's listening comprehension level is almost always higher than his or her independent reading level, Read Alouds can expose students to books of a more complex and sophisticated nature. Thus, when a good book is presented well during a Read Aloud, it can elicit a level of critical thinking and analysis that children would be unable to produce otherwise (Huck, 1979). This benefit is maintained across grades for students in elementary and secondary schools (Butler, 1980).

Teachers have been doing Read Alouds with their students for many decades. However, for years, certain beliefs dictated the methods teachers used; these methods did not engage the students' own thinking processes as keenly as we now understand to be important. In the last decade, a newer kind of Read Aloud has emerged that does indeed allow for more student participation and interaction. In this section, we will first take a look back at more traditional Read Alouds and then examine the interactive Read Aloud.

Presenting a good book well during a Read Aloud encourages stuudents' critical thinking and analysis.

Some Historical Perspective

Lack of During-Reading Interaction

Bedtime story reading has long been considered one of the elements that support literacy development in young children (Holdaway, 1979). Bedtime reading usually means that a fluent reader—typically a caregiver—shares a favorite story out loud with a less fluent reader. As indicated by the term "bedtime reading," this type of reading usually occurs prior to naps or in the evening at bedtime. The context for bedtime reading is often very comfortable and informal, conducted on a sofa, armchair, or perhaps in bed. Such bedtime reading is very similar to what came to be known as the classroom Read Aloud.

For years, many teachers approached the Read Aloud in a limited and fixed way. One survey asked about the amount of time teachers were spending on Read Alouds (Hoffman, Roser, and Battle, 1993). Results indicated that most teachers across elementary grades were spending between 10 and 20 minutes in Read Aloud per day, but of that total amount of time, only 5 minutes was devoted to discussion of the book. Even during the discussions, the amount of time devoted to interaction with and among students was minimal. Clearly, Read Aloud as it was generally implemented for years involved little discussion of the book by the children. Eliminating this element from the Read Aloud greatly reduces the opportunity the child has to fully benefit from the reading experience.

Lack of Perceived Instructional Importance of the Read Aloud

Traditionally, primary-grade teachers have made use of Read Aloud time in their daily schedule but have not viewed it as part of their instruction (Austin and Morrison, 1963). It was usually placed at a point of transition, when students were returning to the room from another activity or getting ready for lunch. The Read Aloud text was usually randomly chosen from what was available in the school library, with little consideration given to how the text might support the teacher's instructional goals.

Intermediate-grade teachers rarely allowed time for class Read Aloud since utilizing every instructional minute was seen as essential. A first-year sixth-grade teacher related the following experience:

TEACHING IN ACTION:
Novice Sixth-Grade Teacher's Experience With Read Alouds

I was never taught to value reading aloud to students as a literacy practice in my teacher preparation program. The focus in the early 1980s was on keeping the students busy with directed literacy activities in their seats. However, intuitively I knew from my own experience as a child that being read to was a very enjoyable experience. I determined to have a Read Aloud time directly after lunch recess. I selected a wonderful, award-winning book (*The Bridge to Terabithia* by Katherine Paterson, 1977) from the school library for the Read Aloud. The students loved being read to, as it helped them to relax before moving on in mathematics activities. I also enjoyed it very much since the students seemed to pay very close attention to my reading of the text.

However, one afternoon, the school principal came into the school during our class Read Aloud time. I could tell by the look on his face that he would be talking to me about this. Sure enough, later that day, I was called to his office where I was informed that we should leave reading for pleasure as an out-of-school activity. I was informed that school was for learning how to read and that does not occur when the students are not busy at work. I learned later on in my career that children really were busy at work during Read Aloud time.

The kind of attitude exemplified here certainly did not encourage many intermediate-grade teachers to read aloud to their students through the 1960s, '70s, and '80s!

One of the reasons for the rejection of the Read Aloud program as an effective literacy strategy in intermediate and secondary schools has been its lack of support for unit or content instruction. In most cases, Read Aloud books were selected for their interest or entertainment value rather than for their connection to the curriculum. This situation, as well as the other problems described above, can be addressed, we've discovered, through a different way of approaching Read Alouds. We characterize this different approach by its key element—interaction.

Interactive Read Alouds

There is general agreement that effective Read Alouds must consist of more than just a teacher reading a book to her students. One key to improving Read Alouds is building in opportunities for students to *respond*. As you design your classroom library, think about how you can use it to foster the following good practices:

> ### Exemplary Read Aloud Characteristics
> (Hoffman, Roser, and Battle, 1993)
>
> ❖ Designate a legitimate time and place in the daily curriculum for reading aloud.
> ❖ Select quality literature.
> ❖ Share literature related to other literature.
> ❖ Discuss literature in lively, invitational, thought-provoking ways.
> ❖ Group children to maximize opportunities to respond.
> ❖ Offer a variety of response and extension opportunities.
> ❖ Reread selected pieces.

Emphasize the Text as Well as the Interaction in an Interactive Read Aloud

In conducting interactive Read Alouds, your primary challenge is to decide when talk is detracting from the text. While a potential criticism of interactive Read Alouds might be that encouraging too much discussion of a book during reading will pull student attention away from some of the aesthetic characteristics of literature, there is another side to this argument. Allowing some discussion during Read Aloud by drawing on student experiences related to the story may actually build the relevance of the activity. Therefore, the goal is to create a balance where individual student experiences related to the text are valued and encouraged without minimizing students' experience of the text itself.

Use Read Alouds to Enhance Knowledge as Well as Provide Enjoyment

As you plan your Read Alouds, remember that they offer a great opportunity to build students' knowledge base as well as their enchantment about books. By reading aloud to your students from information and nonfiction books, you can provide them with additional content instruction, and by focused interaction with them during the Read Alouds you can help strengthen their ability to understand how nonfiction books are structured.

Remember, this requires the classroom library to be the heart of the instructional environment. Students are most able to extend their learning when they have ready access to supportive materials and media, something that effective classroom libraries provide.

Guidelines for Using Interactive Read Alouds

Following are ten helpful guidelines for teachers wishing to use interactive Read Alouds with their students (Barrentine, 1996). As you read them, think about how a well-designed classroom library might enhance your ability to put them to use.

Suggested Guidelines for Interactive Read Alouds

❋ **Carefully select books.** Books with lively characters, rich plots, and creative language are good choices for all grade levels. In addition, for primary grades, books with predictable patterns, high-quality illustrations, and repeated rhythm will help encourage student attention to the text. While multiple readings of a text are appropriate for Read Alouds, introducing new text helps to maintain student interest in this part of the routine. A good place to start is with your favorite books that are also suitable for your students. Since many students will want to do further reading on their own with the selected text or related materials, it's a good idea to place the books in a high-visibility area of the classroom library directly following the Read Aloud.

❋ **Consider the literacy environment.** In order to make the most of interactive Read Alouds, it is important to think carefully about their role vis-à-vis your classroom library and to ask yourself certain questions ahead of time. Will you put all of your books in the classroom library at the beginning of the year or will you hold selected titles back that you will use for interactive Read Alouds? Will you select books that support an instructional theme that is being presented during the same time frame? How will you arrange the children so that they will all be able to see and hear the text being read?

❋ **Prepare for a successful interactive Read Aloud.**

Be thoroughly familiar with the book before the Read Aloud. With picture books, this might mean undertaking several readings of the text before the Read Aloud. With chapter books, it might be necessary to skim the selection you intend to read and familiarize yourself with the structure, plot, problem/resolution, setting, and characters. Be aware of areas of the book that require clarification or enrichment. For instance, one terrific Read Aloud for third to fifth graders, *Superfudge* by Judy Blume, deals with the question of whether there is a Santa Claus and is a good example of why you do not want to be caught off-guard when reading a book aloud to your class!

Think about the goals for reading that you have identified for your students and identify which processes and strategies are at work in your reading of the story. Keep your students in mind as you review the text. What elements in the text need to be expanded on to aid your students in their development as readers? For instance, two excellent Read Alouds for first to third graders, *Miss Rumphius* by Barbara Clooney or *Owl Moon* by Jane Yolen, incorporate flashbacks. For these books, you might want to discuss this technique before reading and, after the reading, ask students to go back to the text and pick out the words that signal flashbacks. When you think about your students' needs as readers, the Read Aloud becomes much more relevant in helping each student benefit from the reading.

Identify where you will encourage students to share predictions about the developing story. Inviting students to make predictions about the story at strategic points in the reading will assist them as they develop an understanding of the text. In a popular Read Aloud picture book, suited for both younger and older children, *Peppe the Lamplighter* by Elisa Bartone, you might stop at the point in the story when Assunta does not come home and ask questions such as: Where might she be? How might Peppe help find her? Allowing class predictions of the story will also support the less able reader in clarifying key information.

Identify where students' background knowledge may be lacking and needing support. It is important to remember that a student's listening comprehension will generally be ahead of his or her reading comprehension. Some concept or vocabulary development ahead of the Read Aloud may help students to interact with stories that they otherwise would not be willing or able to handle. One of the most engaging Read Alouds for third- to sixth-graders, *The Sign of the Seahorse* by Graeme Base, is written as a rhyming play in two acts. The beautiful illustrations help convey the story line, but the language is quite sophisticated. With a book like this, it would be very helpful to preview certain vocabulary and concepts.

Think ahead about how you will phrase questions and use what you observe about students' responses to improve future questions. Learning to ask good questions and to pursue a line of questioning during a discussion is an art in itself. For instance, it is important to ask questions that require the student to think analytically or inferentially, not simply to recall literal-level facts. Likewise, it is important to ask questions based on knowledge or experience that students already have and not on assumptions; undoubtedly, they will not grasp elements of the book at the same level that an adult will. One way to get better at questioning is to observe students' responses carefully so that you gain a better sense of their level of development.

Be flexible and willing to relinquish your plans. Interactive Read Alouds are very dynamic and require a great deal of flexibility on the part of the teacher. Student interactions may add insights that you had not considered previously. Be willing to accept these slight detours as rich additions to the conversation. For example, Louis Sachar's popular *Sideways Stories From Wayside School* (good for grades three through five) contains so many descriptions of odd characters that students probably will be eager to share their own versions of eccentric people they have known or imagined.

Create opportunities for students to explore and extend the book in meaningful ways. It is often appropriate to explore the book in greater detail following the readings. This allows children to achieve greater personalization of the story in their own minds. A book's topic may lead naturally to larger contexts or related subjects. Among the books mentioned above, *Peppe the Lamplighter* lends itself to exploration of the customs, cooking, and languages of ethnic neighborhoods in large cities; *The Sign of the Seahorse* might spur students to research underwater plants and animals or to explore environmental issues; and *Miss Rumphius* could be a means of tapping into students' hopes and plans to better the world when they grow up. A well-designed classroom library will prove a valuable resource as students go off to pursue these kinds of topics and interests.

Where will your Read Aloud fit into the instructional routine? Read Alouds work best if they are built into the daily classroom literacy routine. If they are not integrated into the schedule and planned for, then the chances are good that they will simply not get regular attention. Twenty minutes per day is a general figure for a Read Aloud block. Understand, however, that interactive Read Alouds may take longer depending on the experience of the students.

—Adapted from Barrentine, 1996

Early Language Routine

SETTING: First-Grade Classroom Library
EXAMPLE BOOK: *Take Time to Relax!*
by Nancy Carlson

1. Tune In   (10 Minutes)

This time is dedicated to enjoyment—favorite poems, songs, and jingles, requested by students, are displayed on enlarged text charts and recited or sung. The teacher might also introduce a new piece at this time or perhaps a new activity, such as hand actions, for a familiar piece. Because the book being used for this lesson involves a number of different sports and physical activities (ballet, karate, volleyball, and so on), children might be encouraged to pantomime their favorites.

2. Old Favorites   (10 Minutes)

The children choose an "old favorite"—a story or poem that they have previously enjoyed in the enlarged format. Cloze and masking can be used to encourage predictions. Discussion of words and letters can also take place. This book may or may not relate to the theme or topic of the new book; it is the children's choice.

3. Learning About Language   (15 Minutes)

This is a brief period in which the teacher focuses on a new decoding skill or reviews skills and strategies previously taught that will be useful in the new story. For example, in *Take Time to Relax!*, there are several words that would be challenging for many first graders and that would probably need attention. Or, because the book centrally involves both cause and effect and sequence, these might be excellent strategies to pre-teach or review.

4. New Story   (15 Minutes)

In this segment, either a new story in an enlarged format is introduced or a new story is composed from an old favorite. (This is the main phase in which the LWSL, explained on the next page, is utilized.) The first half of the book *Take Time to Relax!* is set up in a predictable sequence (the days of the week) and should be easy for most children to web (see next page); the second half will prove more challenging but not too difficult for children to ultimately figure out.

5. Independent Reading and Writing   (50 Minutes)

This is the reason for all of the previous activity. Children are now ready for working independently and for engaging in response activities. To ease administration, sometimes this period is subdivided into two segments—reading and writing. Children are expected to make use of the resources in the classroom library and writing center at this point—as they reread the book on their own, find similar books or books by the same author, or write or illustrate their reactions to the story. A book like *Take Time to Relax!*, which has a topic that appeals to most children, humor, and engaging illustrations, should prove an excellent springboard for independent work. There are also a number of other equally enjoyable books by this same author, and students should be encouraged to seek them out in the classroom library.

6. Sharing   (10 Minutes)

Children now share what they have discovered in their independent work. This might mean they read a newly discovered book to a friend or share their writing with the class. These kinds of print interactions will encourage children's willingness to further experiment with language.

—Adapted from Holdaway, 1979

Literature Webbing Strategy Lesson (LWSL) in the Context of the Classroom Library

When we were first-grade teachers, we developed and used a form of interactive Read Aloud (Reutzel and Fawson, 1989) that we called a literature webbing strategy lesson (LWSL). From the start, it was effective in substantially improving students' comprehension of the stories being read and also increasing student engagement.

From its inception, the LWSL has had an active connection to the classroom library. In our own teaching, we pulled about 40 carefully selected book titles out of the classroom library at the beginning of the year to use first during our LWSL instruction. This allowed us to introduce at least one new book each week. By doing this, we were able to use the Read Aloud time to generate a great deal of interest in visiting the classroom library. Each week, there would be at least one new selection making its way back to the library.

In addition, we incorporated children's own writing, as "published" books, into the classroom library collection after each story had been read to the class during author sharing time. We would even place library cards in these books so children could track the frequency with which their books were being read. This provided great encouragement in supporting their continued writing. It also became clear that many children preferred to read their classmates' books rather than other options.

The LWSL was placed in the early literacy routine described in the box on the previous page (Holdaway, 1979) during the "new story" segment. This routine provided an instructional framework through which students' reading and writing activities could be structured and organized. The routine also provided many opportunities for children to engage in active learning. The remaining days of the week allowed the teacher to focus on rereading the children's favorite stories during the "old favorites" segment of the routine.

Within an LWSL, children participate in a variety of interactions with a given text such as *Jump, Frog, Jump!*, which we use as an example text in the model lesson below.

Sample Mini-Lesson

LESSON: *Literature Webbing Strategy Lesson*

Setting: Primary-Grade Classroom Library

Example Book: *Jump, Frog, Jump!* by Robert Kalan

Purpose: To provide support for students as they read this text or related material located in the classroom or write similar stories on their own.

Necessary Supplies/Materials: A copy of the text (ideally in both enlarged and regular formatted text); excerpted predictable text segments placed on cards with representative rebus characters to support emergent readers.

Preparation: Before the lesson begins, the teacher thoroughly reads the book on her own. Then, selected, predictable passages that would allow students to make predictions about the text are excerpted from the book. These passages are written on pieces of paper that are large enough to enable students to easily see the text from their positions on the reading carpet. Next, the title of the book is placed in the center of the chalkboard at the front of the room. The text-excerpt cards are then placed in random order across the bottom of the chalkboard.

Modeling and Instructing:

❖ Encourage student predictions about the book from the cover text and illustrations.

❖ Invite the children to take a brief picture walk of the book. Have them pay close attention to what they see.

❖ Place the book back on display and encourage the children to focus on the text excerpts in the chalkboard tray by reading the text off the cards. Invite the children to place the cards in the order they believe the story unfolds. Encourage discussion about the children's predictions.

❖ While the students look at their predictions for the story on the chalkboard, read the story aloud.

❖ Following the Read Aloud, invite the children to revisit their predictions on the board and make any corrections they feel should be noted.

❖ Read the story again. This time encourage the children to pay close attention to the illustrations and words from the book.

❖ Encourage the children to make final revisions to their predicted order of the book from the text excerpts.

❖ Respond and discuss the content of the book with the children.

❖ Invite students to engage in extensions of the book through interaction with similar books in the classroom library or through writing books on their own with similar patterns.

Monitoring Success: Be aware of students' book and topic choices as they visit the classroom library and participate in writing activities.

The following vignette provides an example of how a literature webbing strategy lesson was presented in one first-grade classroom.

TEACHING IN ACTION:
The Literature Webbing Strategy Lesson in the Context of a First-Grade Classroom Library

The first-grade students in Mrs. Robins' class sat on a rug at the front of the room next to an easel. Mrs. Robins placed a Big Book on the easel. This was a book that she had reserved in her closet for this very moment. It was a new book that she was quite sure most of the children had not yet been exposed to. It was specifically selected for this lesson because it was about big numbers, and Mrs. Robins was introducing some number books into the classroom library. She was confident that this book would encourage a great deal of interest in the new library books.

The children were instantly busy guessing what the book was about from the pictures on the cover. Mrs. Robins read the title, *How Much Is a Million?* (Schwartz, 1985), as she pointed to the words. "What do you think this book is about?" she asked. The children willingly offered their predictions. Then, Mrs. Robins called on several students to recount their predictions. "I think it tells us about a thousand, hundred, million things," the first child related. Another student guessed that it was going to be about how many stars were in space. This was followed by Mrs. Robins taking the children on a quick picture tour of the Big Book. She instructed the children to look at it and think about how it was written.

Next, Mrs. Robins pointed to the title of the book, which she had written in the center of the board. The children recognized the literature web and knew what came next. Out from behind the easel, Mrs. Robins took odd-shaped pieces of posterboard containing handwritten excerpts from the text. She placed these phrases randomly along the chalk tray and said, "I want you to read these together with me and think about how the author might be patterning the story." (See Literature Web, Step 1 illustration on page 64.) "Think about what would make sense first, second, and third in the book." The children read each excerpt together as Mrs. Robins tracked the print with her pointer. As soon as they finished, many students volunteered to explain which part of the book came first and why. This process continued until all of the text excerpts were sequenced around the title of the book, creating a web-like prediction on the board. (See Literature Web, Step 2 illustration on page 65.)

Then Mrs. Robins said, "Listen as I read the story and let's see how we did on our predictions." She began to read. The students' eyes were intently focused on the book during the Read Aloud. As she read, some children focused their attention on the predictions represented in the literature web, making statements like, "Hurray, we got the first one!" or "Too bad. We missed that one." And so it went throughout the reading of the book. When she finished, Mrs. Robins asked them how well they had predicted. "Pretty good," they responded. "We need to fix some of our ideas. That one needs to go second instead of third," said Juan. The discussion continued until all of the predictions were confirmed or corrected. (See Literature Web, Step 3, page 65.)

Finally, Mrs. Robins and the children discussed how the author had written his book. They discovered through careful questioning and teacher guidance that the author had composed it by using a question-and-answer pattern. Mrs. Robins noted that some of the informational books in the classroom library also followed this pattern, and she directed students to generate ideas on how they might extend the information from the text into other areas of the curriculum. Three children were eager to tell Mrs. Robins that they remembered other books that were like this one. The information books they recalled were about trucks, mining, and international airports.

The book was then placed in the listening center for a few days so that the children could revisit the story in a supported setting; afterward, it would be placed in the classroom library where children could check it out and read it independently. Several students expressed interest in doing follow-up projects. With Mrs. Robins' help, they came up with these ideas: counting objects in the classroom to see how high a number they could reach; writing a "Guinness Book of Millions"; and having a discussion about what they each would do with a million dollars.

Following the lesson, Mrs. Robins showed the children other books from the library that present information about numbers:

Anno's Counting Book, Mitsumasa Anno, 1982.

From One to One Hundred, Teri Sloat, 1991.

Mouse Count, Ellen Stoll Walsh, 1991.

Pigs from 1 to 10, Arthur Geisert, 1992.

She briefly introduced these titles and encouraged students to look at the books when they had independent reading and writing time.

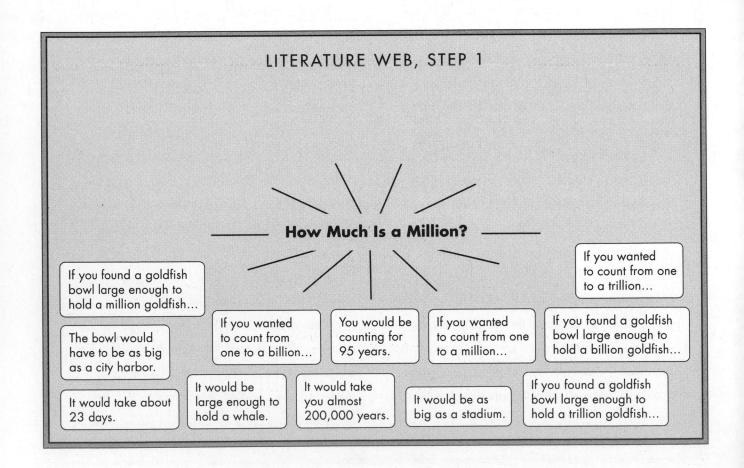

LITERATURE WEB, STEP 1

How Much Is a Million?

If you found a goldfish bowl large enough to hold a million goldfish...

The bowl would have to be as big as a city harbor.

It would take about 23 days.

If you wanted to count from one to a billion...

It would be large enough to hold a whale.

You would be counting for 95 years.

It would take you almost 200,000 years.

If you wanted to count from one to a million...

It would be as big as a stadium.

If you wanted to count from one to a trillion...

If you found a goldfish bowl large enough to hold a billion goldfish...

If you found a goldfish bowl large enough to hold a trillion goldfish...

LITERATURE WEB, STEP 2

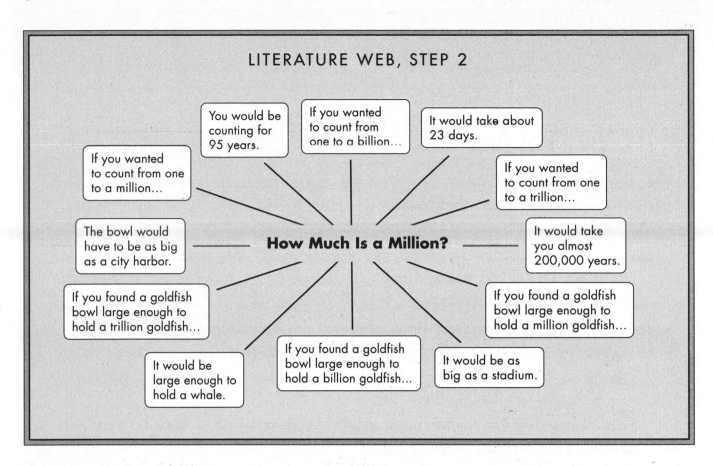

You would be counting for 95 years.

If you wanted to count from one to a billion...

It would take about 23 days.

If you wanted to count from one to a million...

If you wanted to count from one to a trillion...

The bowl would have to be as big as a city harbor.

How Much Is a Million?

It would take you almost 200,000 years.

If you found a goldfish bowl large enough to hold a trillion goldfish...

If you found a goldfish bowl large enough to hold a million goldfish...

It would be large enough to hold a whale.

If you found a goldfish bowl large enough to hold a billion goldfish...

It would be as big as a stadium.

LITERATURE WEB, STEP 3

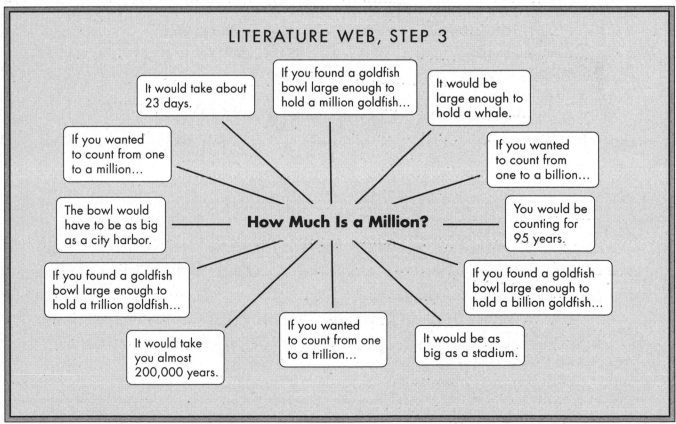

It would take about 23 days.

If you found a goldfish bowl large enough to hold a million goldfish...

It would be large enough to hold a whale.

If you wanted to count from one to a million...

If you wanted to count from one to a billion...

The bowl would have to be as big as a city harbor.

How Much Is a Million?

You would be counting for 95 years.

If you found a goldfish bowl large enough to hold a trillion goldfish...

If you found a goldfish bowl large enough to hold a billion goldfish...

It would take you almost 200,000 years.

If you wanted to count from one to a trillion...

It would be as big as a stadium.

The following vignette provides an example of how an interactive Read Aloud lesson was presented in one fifth-grade classroom.

TEACHING IN ACTION:
An Interactive Read Aloud in the Context of a Fifth-Grade Classroom Library

Mr. Sanchez had decided to use the story *Wringer* (Spinelli, 1997) as a class Read Aloud for his fifth graders. Because it was a Level U book, about average difficulty for fifth-grade readers, he felt it was a good choice. For the struggling readers in his class, it would mean supported reading of a challenging text. And the story itself was appropriate because it would allow his students to explore some of the emotions and issues of pre- and early adolescence, such as personal identity and how to relate to peers.

To encourage student engagement and interaction, Mr. Sanchez chose a Read Aloud framework that would involve his students in before, during, and post reading activities. He selected a pre-reading activity that was aimed at helping students better understand their own perceptions about friends; it involved an exploration of the general characteristics of good and bad friends. During the Read Aloud, students would be asked to evaluate the various characters in the story. Following the reading of the book, Mr. Sanchez would invite the students to generate literary "report cards" for the book and to compare *Wringer* to other fiction books with the same theme in the classroom library.

Mr. Sanchez began the Read Aloud by having each student contribute an attribute to a chart on characteristics of good friends and bad friends. Together, they created the following chart:

Good Friend	Bad Friend
1. Asks you to play.	1. Doesn't invite you to play.
2. Doesn't lie to you.	2. Teases you.
3. Likes some of the things you like.	3. Tells you lies.
4. Is able to keep a secret.	4. Takes your lunch money.
5.	5.
6.	6.
7.	7.

Mr. Sanchez then instructed the students to pay close attention as he read *Wringer* aloud to consider both how the character Palmer was influenced by his friends and what kinds of friends these really were. On the first day, he read Chapter 1 and discussed the term *wringer*, which was unfamiliar to many students.

Prior to beginning the Read Aloud for Chapter 2 the following day, Mr. Sanchez provided each student with a character map grid. As the book was read and character names mentioned, they were to place one main character and his or her attributes in each box.

Palmer (Snots)	Beans	Mutto	Henry	Dorothy (Fishface)

At the conclusion of each chapter, Mr. Sanchez and the students discussed any new information about the main characters in the story. Students were also asked periodically to explain why Palmer's friends were good or bad.

At the end of the story, Mr. Sanchez involved his students in a lively discussion of the story and how they related to the various characters. Finally, Mr. Sanchez grouped the students in pairs. Each student pair was given a report card for the book. Together, students provided a letter grade for each of the items listed on the card. Student responses were then shared and discussed with the whole class.

Waymer Elementary School
Student: Palmer

Area	Grade	Reason
Physical Education	A	He ran fast to get away from Beans, Mutto, and Henry
Creativity	A	He was able to hide Nipper very well.
Respect for others	D	Palmer was very rude to Dorothy.
Responsibility	B	He took good care of Nipper but should have told his parents what was happening.
Honesty	D	Palmer should not have lied to Dorothy and his parents about Nipper or the way his friends were treating him. He also should have been honest about not wanting to be a wringer.

In the next weeks, Mr. Sanchez set up a prominent display in the classroom library that featured several copies of *Wringer* alongside the students' literary report cards. He also displayed related books about friendship by authors such as Judy Blume, Beverly Cleary, and Gary Paulsen, as well as a few of Jerry Spinelli's other books—*Maniac McGee* and *Star Girl*. From past experience, Mr. Sanchez was not surprised to see that every book in the display got checked out at least once in the month following the Read Aloud.

Helpful Tips for Conducting Interactive Read Alouds: A Checklist

We conclude this chapter with a checklist of tips for you to use in conducting Read Alouds in your own classroom.

A Teacher's Checklist for Effective Read Alouds

❖ Choose books that are interesting and engaging.

❖ Read to children every day for at least 20 minutes.

❖ Provide access to Read Aloud materials for individual use in the classroom library.

❖ Involve all children when reading aloud. Reading to children is a critical part of helping struggling readers develop language and become readers themselves.

❖ In the primary grades, read several books a day so that children get used to hearing rich language, various text structures, and a variety of genres.

❖ In the intermediate grades, choose books that will maintain students' interest from chapter to chapter. Suspenseful books, books that build steadily to a climax, or books that pose a real-life moral dilemma are good choices. (At the end of this checklist, you'll find some of our recommendations for both primary- and intermediate-grade Read Alouds. These books are particularly suited to being read aloud.)

❖ For all grades, read some selections that reflect cultural diversity. Highlight these and related selections in displays within the classroom library.

❖ Know the books well so that children hear an excellent model of oral reading.

❖ Invite other people to read to the children from time to time. You may want to ask the school principal, the custodian, the secretary, parents, citizens, city officials, and police officers.

❖ Make sure you have established parameters for Read Aloud time. Each teacher is different— be sure to help students understand what they can and cannot do while you are reading.

❖ You may want to preface reading with an attention-grabbing statement to engage children in listening before you begin reading. For example, for the book *Animals Should Definitely Not Wear Clothing* (Barrett, 1970), you might start off your Read Aloud by describing for students the strangest animal you've ever seen (or imagined) or for an Amelia Bedelia book (Peggy Paris), you might launch off with a tongue twister, nonsense words, or other humorous examples of wordplay.

❖ Assess prior knowledge and fill in information for children who need it to better understand the story.

❖ Set a purpose for reading. For instance, if you were about to read aloud *The Little Prince* (de Saint Exupery, 1943) to your fourth or fifth graders, you might have them try to figure out the lessons behind this book's simple fantasy tale.

❖ Relate new Read Alouds to familiar stories students have accessed in the classroom, at home, or in school collections.

❖ Try to keep the pages facing the children so they can see the illustrations.

❖ When reading chapter books, show the children any illustrations.

* Prearrange a strategic stopping point in chapter books so children anticipate hearing the rest of the book.

* Use a variety of dramatic strategies to engage listeners in the story. For instance, you might use a special "storytelling apron" with many pockets, from which you pull—at appropriate moments in the story—just the right prop or felt character. (See photo at right for one example of a storytelling apron.)

* Use any opportunities for learning and making connections to other topics students are studying. Support these topics with special collections in the classroom library. But don't interrupt the story to the point that it interferes with comprehension.

* After reading, be sure to allow students the opportunity to discuss and ask questions. It may be appropriate from time to time to ask children to think aloud, which assists in comprehension.

* Engage students in author studies, especially authors of multiple-title collections. (See lists in Chapters 1 and 4 for recommended series books.)

A Sampling of Great Read Alouds for Your Classroom Library

PRIMARY

* George and Martha series, James Marshall

* Frog and Toad series, Arnold Lobel

* Amelia Bedelia series, Peggy Parish

* Curious George series, H. A. Rey

* *Alexander and the Terrible, Horrible, No Good, Very Bad Day*, Judith Viorst

* *Where the Wild Things Are*, Maurice Sendak

INTERMEDIATE

* *The Midnight Fox*, Betsy Byars

* *Tales of a Fourth-Grade Nothing*, Judy Blume

* *Hatchet*, Gary Paulsen

* *My Brother Sam Is Dead*, James Lincoln Collier and Christopher Collier

* *Sideways Stories from Wayside School*, Louis Sachar

* *Holes*, Louis Sachar

* *The Lion, the Witch, and the Wardrobe*, C. S. Lewis

CHAPTER 3: How Does the Classroom Library Support Reading *to* Children?

69

CHAPTER 4

How Does the Classroom Library Support Reading *With* Children?

Gathering his sixth graders together, Mr. Sanchez has them sit around a small table in the classroom library. They have chosen to read *Bridge to Terabithia* by Katherine Paterson. They begin this guided reading lesson with a teacher-led discussion. Mr. Sanchez asks if any of the children have "getaway" places where they go to escape and dream. Jill says she and her friends go to her bedroom, close the door, and talk. Austin says he and his friends go to the local park and climb a favorite oak tree where they sit on the branches to talk and dream. Mr. Sanchez reminds his students, "Having friends you trust and can talk to is very important. But having a place where you can always go to talk and dream without worry is also wonderful." Mr. Sanchez points out that in this book, young friends find an almost magical place, across a small bridge over a clear brook, where they can imagine, talk, and dream. But as time goes on something tragic happens in this unique place they called Terabithia.

Reading *with* children is a vital part of an effective, comprehensive reading program. As you read with your students, you are uniquely able to demonstrate and guide them into strategies for successfully processing the print on the page (Mooney, 1990). And, as Mr. Sanchez has discovered, a well-stocked and well-organized classroom library can provide the instructional space and the right books for a teacher to engage in shared reading, guided reading, and other reading instruction with students.

Use Your Classroom Library to Make Shared Reading Come Alive

What Is *Shared Reading*?

Shared reading is intended to help teachers replicate in the classroom all of the important characteristics of bedtime or lap-reading (Holdaway, 1979, 1981). Sometimes called the *shared book experience*, it is used with very young readers to model the reading process for an entire group of children. There is really only one key modification that needs to be made for an entire classroom to share a book: The print needs to be enlarged so that

every child can see it and process it at the same time under the guidance of the teacher (Barrett, 1982).

When selecting books or stories for shared reading experiences, try to find those most loved by children. Any book or story (including selections in basal readers) that you intend to read with children during shared reading should have literary merit, engaging content, and high interest. The illustrations must augment and expand on the text, and they should support

In shared reading, the teacher models the reading process for a large group of young readers.

the reading of the story in proper sequence. These books and stories are best if they contain repetition, cumulative sequence, rhyme, and rhythm to entice children into the melody and cadence of words. Such books hook children on the sounds and patterns of language.

Books like *Brown Bear, Brown Bear* or *Polar Bear, Polar Bear* by Bill Martin (1990, 1991) are ideal initial books for shared reading. For one thing, they put reasonable demands on younger readers' capabilities. It is very important that the number of unknown words in a shared reading book does not overburden emerging readers. And it is also helpful for very young readers that the pictures carry the storyline. As in Bill Martin's books, the print may amount to little more than a caption underneath the pictures.

As children become acquainted with more words, select books in which the print and the picture carry a more equal share of the story's message—such as *The Gingerbread Man* (Schmidt), *I Know an Old Lady* (Bonne), and *The Grouchy Lady Bug* (Carle). Eventually, you will be able to use books in which the print carries the story and the illustrations simply complement the text. Good examples of these kinds of books include *Mailing May* (Tunnell), *Mike Mulligan and His Steam Shovel* (Burton), and *Albert's Toothache* (Williams). Remember, books chosen for shared reading experiences need to have the same visual impact on 20 to 25 children that a standard-sized book would have on a child seated in a parent's lap. This requirement typically means that teachers will need to use Big Books (commercially available books that are usually constructed of poster-size cardboard); enlarged print on chart paper; overheads; or CD-ROM books projected onto a screen. You can also use multiple copies of the same book or story in small group settings.

When these conditions for book selection are met, children and teachers truly share the reading experience. They share the discovery of good books, an awareness of how print works, and the power of language. What's more, children gain a growing confidence in their ability to read (Barrett, 1982).

How to Conduct a Shared Reading or Shared Book Experience

Begin a shared book experience by introducing the book. An introduction is intended to heighten children's desire to read the story and to help them draw on their own experiences and prior knowledge.

Invite children to look at the book cover. For example, let's say you have selected Eric Carle's *The Very Hungry Caterpillar* (an excellent choice for an early shared book experience). Undoubtedly, the first thing students will notice is the caterpillar. You can draw them in further by asking what they think the caterpillar is doing and what he will do in this book, guiding them toward the idea that he is hungry. This will prepare them for the title, which you then read aloud. Next you can talk about the front and back of the book and point out certain features, such as author and illustrator names, publisher, copyright date, and title page.

Then you might ask the students to look at the pictures and ask, "What do you think the words will tell you?" This request typically opens up a discussion leading to personal connections and prediction. For this book, children will likely talk about personal experiences involving cocoons, moths, or butterflies. After that, the goal is to read the book with "full dramatic punch, perhaps overdoing a little some of the best parts" (Barrett, 1982). While reading the story, invite children to join in on any repeated or predictable phrases or words. At key points, you should pause to encourage students to predict what is coming next in the story. Carle's story, with its progression through the days of the week and through the caterpillar's daily increasing diet, lends itself naturally to repetition and predictions.

After the reading, invite children to share their responses to the story. Encourage them to talk about their favorite parts. You might immediately reread the book, this time asking students to use hand and body movements or rhythm instruments to depict the story. When we used *The Very Hungry Caterpillar*, students spontaneously "chomped" at the end of each page where the caterpillar was eating something, and waved their arms like wings at the end of the book to show the butterfly flying away.

End your shared book experience by telling students that the book is now back in the classroom library. We guarantee that it will eventually become part of a selection of favorite stories that are read again and again.

Put the Classroom Library at the Core of Shared Reading

When you return a book to the classroom library after a shared reading experience, don't just put it back—put it on display. You can use easels, the tops of bookshelves, tabletops, chalkboard trays, or rain gutters affixed to the tops of bookshelves. These displays are bound to attract student interest, and interest motivates students to select these shared reading materials for independent rereading. With practice, these shared reading books often become young readers' favorites.

In addition to these featured displays, the classroom library provides the ideal location for storing Big Books and multiple copies of traditional-sized books, as well as for displaying charts and other enlarged print products used for shared reading.

Storage of Big Books presents a challenge. There are a number of arrangements you can set up for storing them efficiently:

❀ Use pants hangers for display and storage.

❀ Use appropriately sized and labeled bins.

❀ Create special shelving, such as large pockets (see photo at right).

Small plastic baskets are ideal for storing multiple copies of individual titles of traditional-sized books. If finances or space present problems in obtaining baskets, collect used breakfast cereal boxes, snip the tops off, and cut the boxes at a 45-degree angle—a method we've used successfully. Multiple copies of individual titles can be placed into these cereal boxes and labeled to keep them together in a single spot.

Following is a summary of the major ways in which the classroom library can help you develop and maintain the shared reading component of your classroom reading program:

❀ Shared reading books can be stored in a specific location, identified and labeled for that purpose.

❀ The library can have a listening center that includes a tape

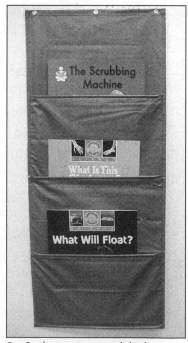

Big Books require special display areas, such as these large pockets.

recorder with several headphones, multiple small copies of the shared reading Big Book, and a tape recording of the shared reading book.

☀ A computer with a CD-ROM version of the Big Book story that you've just read is great for supported rereadings in the library.

☀ The classroom library is an ideal spot for providing supported practice through rereading the shared reading book with a small group of children.

The classroom library often includes a listening center, allowing students to hear a tape recording of a shared reading book.

☀ The library is also an ideal place for two or more children to select Big Books for rereading during independent reading time.

Use Your Classroom Library to Make Guided Reading Come Alive

Guided reading is an essential part of a comprehensive reading program. It supports two major instructional purposes: (1) to develop reading strategies; and (2) to move children toward independent reading. Guided reading involves the use of leveled books that present too many challenges for children to read on their own initially (Mooney, 1990; Fountas and Pinnell, 1996, 2001).

Children should be introduced to guided reading only after they have had ample opportunities to listen to stories, poems, songs, and so forth and to participate in shared reading experiences. Using an established lesson pattern based on a careful study of the text itself, the teacher quite literally guides the children through the reading. Guided reading instruction is intended to focus on helping children in the "zone of their proximal development" (Vygotsky, 1978), or at that point in their development where they can succeed at a certain task with some expert help but not yet on their own. It is provided in a small-group setting; the groups are composed of children who reflect a similar range of competencies, experiences, and interests (Mooney, 1990; Fountas and Pinnell, 1996, 2001).

A great deal of research and writing about guided reading instruction is available, but it is not our purpose in this book to discuss it in depth. Instead, we refer you to two good sources of pragmatic information, *Guided Reading: Making It Work* (Schulman and Payne) and *Literacy: Helping Children Construct Meaning* (Cooper, 2001). Here we summarize some basic instructional frameworks and then move on to what *does* concern us: the books you can use in your instruction and the central role your classroom library can play in reading instruction.

CHAPTER 4: How Does the Classroom Library Support Reading *With* Children?

75

Primary Grades

There are seven phases of a primary-grade guided reading lesson:

Picture Walk-Talk: Teacher guides children through pictures of a new book.

First Reading: Teacher does an initial reading until children develop greater reading abilities.

Language Play: Lessons around a close reading of the text focus on text elements—words, sentence structure, layout, and so on—that may present challenges.

Rereading: Children reread the text aloud (or silently as they develop oral fluency) while the teacher listens in on each child's quiet oral rereading.

Retelling: Children take turns retelling each other and/or the teacher what they have read. They come to understand that stories have a beginning, middle, and end.

Sharing Competence: Children take the guided reading texts home to share with parents, caregivers, or siblings.

Extending Meaning: Children engage in projects that extend their understanding of the texts through storytelling, puppetry, plays, murals, and hand actions.

Intermediate Grades

As children develop increasing fluency and expanding interests in the intermediate years, reading instruction changes along with them. All of the activities associated with guiding reading in these years are intended to sharpen and refine children's reading fluency and critical thinking skills (Fountas and Pinnell, 2001; Reutzel and Cooter, 1991, 2000).

At this level, we believe the *reading workshop* (Atwell, 1987; Reutzel and Cooter, 1991; Fountas and Pinnell, 2001) best provides a functional, flexible instructional and organizational framework for reading instruction. It is also a framework that incorporates full use of a classroom library. The format for the reading workshop that we recommend has five parts: (1) teacher sharing time; (2) a mini-lesson; (3) state of the class (evaluation and monitoring of students); (4) workshop, including independent reading or sustained silent reading (SSR), literature response groups, and literature circles; and (5) student sharing time. There are a number of exciting ways in which you can utilize your classroom library books and resources within this framework, especially within the mini-lessons, literature response groups, and literature circles. Some examples appear a bit later in this chapter.

At these grade levels, instruction is also aimed at helping students develop as writers—to hone their ability to read as writers—and at deepening their appreciation for language. Because these goals are so important, writing instruction is typically built into the intermediate-grade instructional framework. At the end of the chapter, we'll show you how you can use your classroom library to focus on writing, as well as to reinforce key reading strategy instruction when necessary.

Gather Guided Reading Books to Provide That "Just Right" Match

The most important consideration in forming guided reading groups is to match children in the group with "just right" books—books they cannot read independently without some guidance from the teacher. A well-planned and well-stocked classroom library will be a tremendous aid. If you give consideration early in the year to the kinds of books you need to have available for guided reading, and if you arrange these books by level, you will be more prepared to engage your students in guided reading instruction when the time is right.

Guided reading groups change as children progress through the year. "Just right" books should present children with a reasonable challenge, but also with a high degree of potential for success. This means that children should, without help, be able to read approximately 90 percent of the words in a book selected for a guided reading group. Books used for initial guided reading experiences should demonstrate all of the following:

❈ A close match of text and pictures

❈ Gradual introduction of unfamiliar concepts and words

❈ Sufficient repetition of predictable elements

Primary-Grade Leveled Books

Based on the ideas of Fountas and Pinnell (1996, 1999), we have constructed a text gradient summary by grade level (presented below) for selecting reading books to provide the "just right" match for children. The list will be more helpful to you if you also use the graph that follows it to interpret the meaning of each level. You'll also find book titles accompanying each level; these are recommended representative titles for a particular level. They're just a beginning, of course. You can have some real fun browsing among the many excellent children's literature titles and trade books now available to create your own lists.

Leveling Criteria for Books, Levels A–P

(Note: Each level incorporates the features of the preceding level and builds upon it.)

LEVELS A–B

❈ There is a single idea or storyline.

❈ Pictures and text are interdependent to carry the story.

❈ Topics are familiar to children's experiences.

❈ Texts use natural oral-language structures.

❈ Print and layout are consistent and easy to follow.

❈ Print is separate from pictures.

❈ Texts use the full range of punctuation.

❈ Spacing is sufficient to easily determine word boundaries.

❈ Words are repeated throughout the story.

❈ Pages contain one to four lines of print, with Level A having fewer and Level B more.

A

Underwater, Rebel Williams
I Like to Find Things, Gavin Bishop
Dogs, Amy Levin
Painting, Joy Cowley

CHAPTER 4: How Does the Classroom Library Support Reading *With* Children?

77

Moms & Dads, Beverly Randell, Jenny Giles, and
　　Annette Smith

B

Hats Around the World, Liza Charlesworth
Making Mountains, Margaret Ballinger and
　　Rachel Gossett
For Breakfast, Patricia T. Cousin, Claudette C.
　　Mitchell, and Gracie R. Porter
Here I Am, Judy Nayer
Sally's New Shoes, Annette Smith

LEVEL C

* Pages contain two to five lines each.

* Story is carried more by the print than the
　pictures, but pictures remain important.

* Print may carry across a two-page layout in
　columns.

* Sentences are longer.

* More words are used.

C

At the Store, Patricia T. Cousin, Claudette C.
　　Mitchell, and Gracie R. Porter
One for You and One for Me, Wendy Blaxland
In the City, Susan Pasternac
Bo and Peter, Betsy Franco
Fishing, Annette Smith

LEVEL D

* Stories still simple but storyline is more complex.

* Pictures are still important but story is
　increasingly based on the print.

* Pages contain up to six lines of print per page.

* Sentences are longer.

* Texts use more words, including those with
　inflected endings.

D

The Ball Game, David Packard
Hide and Seek, Roberta Brown and Sue Carey
Where We Live, Brenda Parkes
The Farm Concert, Joy Cowley
Lizard Loses Its Tail, Beverly Randell

LEVEL E

* Pages contain up to eight lines of print per page.

* Placement of text on the page may begin to vary.

* Pictures contain several ideas and the text carries
　the story.

* Problem solving is needed to connect text and
　pictures.

* Words require a greater degree of word analysis
　skills.

* Concepts in the story may be less familiar to
　children.

* Longer stories have more words.

E

The Rain and the Sun, Allan Trussell-Cullen
Which Hat Today?, Margaret Ballinger and Rachel
　　Gossett
The Red Rose, Joy Cowley
My Dad's Truck, Meredith Costain
Tortillas, Margarita Gonzelez-Jensen

LEVEL F

* Print is smaller.

* Literary language is mixed with oral-language
　patterns.

* Frequently used words are expanded in the stories.

* Stories have a distinct beginning, middle, and end.

* Use of dialogue increases.

* Word-analysis skills are increasingly needed at
　this level.

F

My Very Hungry Pet, Debbie Swan
The Best Thing About Food, Fay Robinson
The Jigaree, Joy Cowley
Late for Soccer, Jeremy Giles
Tabby in the Tree, Beverly Randell

LEVELS G & H

* Ideas and vocabulary are more challenging.

* Content is increasingly distant from children's
　experiences.

* Stories contain repeated language patterns in
　multiple episodes.

* Stories are longer with more pages per book than
　in previous levels.

* Repetition within episodes becomes less in level H
　books.

G

Knobby Knuckles, Knobby Knees, Jill Carter and
  Judy Ling
How Have I Grown?, Mary Reid
Balcony Garden, Rebecca Weber
Grandpa's Lemonade, Helen Upson
William's Skateboard, Dale Golder

H

Mom's Secret, Meredith Costain
I Was Walking Down the Road, Sarah Barchas
Digging to China, Katherine Goldsby
Robert and the Rocket, Leesa Waldron
George Shrinks, William Noyce

LEVEL I

❊ Texts are of greater variety, including
  information texts.

❊ Story structure is more complex, with more
  episodes and with themes less related to
  experiences of children.

❊ Point of view is introduced.

❊ Texts increase in length, and there are more
  than eight sentences per page.

❊ Texts include large numbers of unfamiliar words
  requiring word analysis skills.

I

Dancin' Down, Evangeline Nicholas
The Friendly Crocodile, Monica Hiris
Swimming Lessons, Amy Algie
Big Bad Rex, Betty Erickson
The Witch's Haircut, Mavis Wyvill

LEVEL J

❊ Variety of genre increases.

❊ Books are 30 to 60 pages in length.

❊ Chapter books start at this level.

❊ Longer books have easier text to sustain interest.

❊ Shorter books have more difficult text, requiring
  greater word analysis and interpretive abilities.

❊ Character development is enhanced in these
  texts.

J

Stone Soup, Ann McGovern
Dolphins, Marion Rego

There's an Alligator Under My Bed, Mercer Mayer
King Midas and the Golden Touch, Allan Trussell-
  Cullen
Children of Sierra Leone, Arma Christiana

LEVEL K

❊ Easy chapter books have a picture on each or
  every other page.

❊ Text is relatively easy in these books, helping
  children sustain the reading of longer books.

❊ Literary picture books at this level have about
  15 lines per page.

❊ Oral reading is now moving toward more silent
  reading.

K

Buffalo Bill and the Pony Express, Elenor Coerr
Keep the Lights Burning, Abbie, Peter and
  Connie Roop
More Tales of Oliver Pig, Jean V. Leeuwen
Nate the Great Goes Undercover, Marjorie W.
  Sharmat

LEVEL L

❊ Picture books are longer and more complex.

❊ Chapter books involve more complex plots that
  span longer periods of time.

❊ Texts represent a full range of genres.

❊ Most chapter books are 70 to 80 pages long.

❊ Print size is varied and often smaller.

L

Happy Birthday, Martin Luther King, Jean Marzollo
Katy and the Big Snow, Virginia L. Burton
The Littles, John Peterson
Teach Us, Amelia Bedelia, Peggy Parish

LEVEL M

❊ Chapter books are longer with fewer pictures.

❊ Themes and topics vary widely and are more
  complex.

❊ Print size is smaller with more lines and words
  per page.

❊ Ancillary information materials may be
  included, such as maps, glossaries, vignettes,
  biographies, and time lines.

 CHAPTER 4: How Does the Classroom Library Support Reading *With* Children?

79

M

Amazing Grace, Mary Hoffman and Caroline Binch
Blueberries for Sal, Robert McCloskey
Cloudy With a Chance of Meatballs, Judi Barrett
Kate Shelley and the Midnight Express,
    Margaret K. Wetterer
Blue Ribbon Blues, Jerry Spinelli
Ghost Town Treasure, Clyde Robert Bulla
Vampires Don't Wear Polka Dots, Debbie Dady and
    Marcia Thornton Jones

LEVEL N

❋ Books are 100 pages or more.

❋ Chapters are 15 to 20 pages in length.

❋ More emphasis is placed on reading informational
   texts.

❋ Texts still have one plot and episodic structures.

❋ Books require a cultural or historical context for
   interpretation.

N

Rumpelstiltskin, Paul O. Zelinsky
Lion Dance, Kate Waters and Madeline Slovenz-Low
The Most Wonderful Doll in the World,
    Phyllis McGinley
We'll Never Forget You, Roberto Clemente,
    Trudie Engel
Max Malone Makes a Million, Charlotte Herman
Squanto: Friend of the Pilgrims, Clyde Robert Bulla

LEVEL O

❋ Texts have multiple characters with interwoven
   plots, flashbacks, or other complex writing styles.

❋ Longer books have up to 200 pages and include
   realistic fiction, biographies, science fiction, and
   folk and fairy tales.

❋ Illustrations are primarily black and white but are
   used infrequently.

❋ Many new multisyllable words are used.

O

Gladly Here I Come, Joy Cowley
The Mouse and the Motorcycle, Beverly Cleary
The Bad Dad List, Anna Kenna
The Sock Gobbler and Other Stories, Barbara Berge
E Is for Elisa, Johanna Hurwitz
Henry and Ribsy, Beverly Cleary

Ramona Forever, Beverly Cleary

LEVEL P

❋ Figurative language is used but explained by the
   writer.

❋ Texts are longer and more complex, with greater
   variety of types and genre.

❋ Texts are largely distanced from the children's
   personal experiences, requiring greater ability to
   understand historical contexts and interpret new
   meanings from the text.

P

The T.F. Letters, Karen Ray
A Taste of Blackberries, Doris B. George
The Private Notebook of Katie Roberts, Sonja Lamut
Justin and the Best Biscuits in the World, Mildred P.
    Walter
The Forgotten Door, Alexander Key

—Based on Fountas and Pinnell, 1999

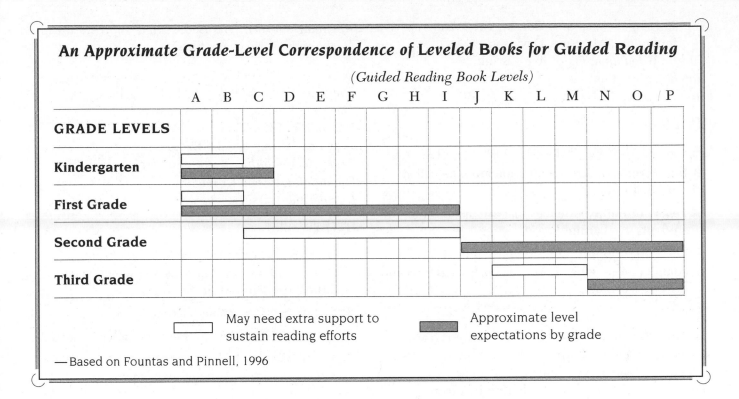

An Approximate Grade-Level Correspondence of Leveled Books for Guided Reading

(Guided Reading Book Levels)

A B C D E F G H I J K L M N O / P

GRADE LEVELS

Kindergarten

First Grade

Second Grade

Third Grade

☐ May need extra support to sustain reading efforts

■ Approximate level expectations by grade

—Based on Fountas and Pinnell, 1996

Intermediate-Grade Leveled Books

The same leveling gradient was applied to intermediate-grade books (Fountas and Pinnell, 2001) so that teachers of grades four through six can make the same informed choices for selecting guided reading books (Daniels, 1994). Again, as with the primary-grade lists, each level incorporates and builds upon the attributes of the previous level. And again, the titles we offer here are but a suggestion and a springboard for your own classroom library selections. A graph for the intermediate grade follows the list.

LEVEL Q

❈ These books have very few illustrations.

❈ Books employ more complex sentences and vocabulary than previous levels.

❈ Plots are complex, offering sophisticated humor and interesting ideas.

❈ Characterization is shown through the use of dialogue and perspective.

❈ Books are quite long, requiring sustained interest and reading over many days.

❈ Books may focus on mature themes associated with problems in society.

Q

Run Away From Home, Patricia C. McKissack
The Great Brain Does It Again, John D. Fitzgerald
Sara Crewe, Frances H. Burnett
The Story of George Washington Carver, Eva Moore
Bunnicula, James Howe
James and the Giant Peach, Roald Dahl
Superfudge, Judy Blume

LEVEL R

❈ Books represent a range of times in history.

❈ Vocabulary requires understanding of connotative meanings.

❈ Fiction books may use simile and metaphor.

❈ Nonfiction books focus on biographies and autobiographies.

❈ Books may deal with mature themes such as war, family problems, and death.

R

Fourth Grade Rats, Jerry Spinelli
Sounder, William Armstrong
The Best, Worst School Year Ever, Barbara Robinson

CHAPTER 4: How Does the Classroom Library Support Reading *With* Children?

❮ **81** ❯

The Story of Thomas Alva Edison: The Wizard of Menlo Park, Margaret Davidson
Caddie Woodlawn, Carol Ryrie Brink
Hatchet, Gary Paulsen
Shiloh, Phyllis R. Naylor

LEVEL S

❋ Books reflect a wide variety of topics and cultures.

❋ Many works of historical fiction are included at this level.

❋ Texts present experiences that are distant from the students' background.

❋ Texts offer opportunities to make inter-textual connections among other previously read texts and historical events.

There's a Boy in the Girls' Bathroom, Louis Sachar
Little House on the Prairie, Laura I. Wilder
Stone Fox, John R. Gardiner
The Great Gilly Hopkins, Katherine Paterson
The Borrowers, Mary Norton
Matilda, Roald Dahl

LEVEL T

❋ Texts use many multisyllable words.

❋ Texts use a variety of structures and genres.

❋ Fantasy, historical fiction, information, biographies, and realistic fiction are all part of this level.

❋ Themes at this level include growing up, courage, hardship, and prejudice.

❋ Texts deal with different cultural and racial groups.

T

The Chronicles of Narnia, C. S. Lewis
Old Yeller, Fred Gipson
The Red Pony, John Steinbeck
Danny, Champion of the World, Roald Dahl
My Hiroshima, Junko Morimoto

LEVEL U

❋ Texts present information with specific technical structures, such as charts, graphs, and tables.

❋ Narrative texts are complex, with plots and subplots.

❋ Characters are multidimensional and complex.

❋ Themes are more abstract and writers use symbolism.

❋ Creative formats are used, such as short stories all about the same character(s).

The View From Saturday, E. L. Konigsburg
The Long Winter, Laura I. Wilder
Julie of the Wolves, Jean C. George
Tuck Everlasting, Natalie Babbitt
Bridge to Terabithia, Katherine Paterson
Onion John, Joseph Krumgold
Number the Stars, Lois Lowry

LEVEL V

❋ Biographies at this level include significant coverage of historical fact, harsh themes, and difficult periods of history.

❋ Fiction includes science fiction.

❋ Texts require readers to think critically.

❋ Size of print is smaller, and texts may have 200 to 300 pages with many more words per page.

V

Harry Potter series, J. K. Rowling
Maniac McGee, Jerry Spinelli
Anne of Green Gables, L. M. Montgomery
Mrs. Frisby and the Rats of NIHM, Robert C. O'Brien
Island of the Blue Dolphins, Scott O'Dell
A Wrinkle in Time, Madeline L'Engle

LEVEL W

❋ Texts require an awareness of social and political issues.

❋ Fantasy and science fiction introduce heroic characters, moral questions, and contests between good and evil.

❋ Information books have increasingly complex technical information.

❋ Biographies have many details prompting readers to make inferences about characters' motivations.

I Am a Star: Child of the Holocaust, Inge Auerbacher
The Phantom Tollbooth, Norton Juster
Stowaway, Karen Hesse
After the Dancing Days, Margaret I. Rostkowski
The Star Fisher, Lawrence Yep

LEVEL X

❋ Science fiction includes technical information as well as high fantasy.

❋ Readers must go beyond the literal level to construct meaning.

❋ Sophistication of vocabulary, language, and topic continues to increase.

LEVEL Y

❋ Books present subtle themes and complex plots.

❋ Texts include irony and satire.

❋ Works include heroic figures and heroic journeys,

❋ Texts must be analyzed for underlying messages and for traditional plot elements.

LEVEL Z

❋ Information books deal with controversial social concepts and political issues.

❋ Readers learn new strategies for finding technical information.

❋ Narratives provide graphic details of violence and hardship.

❋ Texts provide a great deal of highly technical information.

XYZ

Where the Red Fern Grows, Wilson Rawls
Memories of Anne Frank, Alison L. Gold
The Diary of a Young Girl, Anne Frank
Novio Boy, Gary Soto
Call It Courage, Armstrong Sperry
Carry On, Mr. Bowditch, Jean Lee Latham
Sacajawea, Joseph Bruchac
The Giver, Lois Lowry
My Brother Sam Is Dead, James and Christopher Collier
White Fang, Jack London
A Day No Pigs Would Die, Sylvia Peck
The Hobbit, J. R. R. Tolkien
Adventures of Huck Finn, Mark Twain
Treasure Island, Robert Louis Stevenson

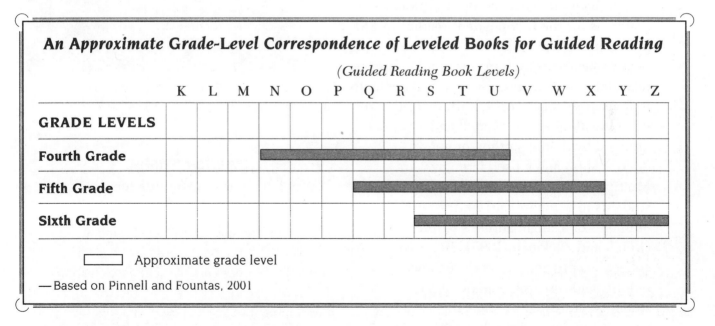

An Approximate Grade-Level Correspondence of Leveled Books for Guided Reading

(Guided Reading Book Levels)

	K	L	M	N	O	P	Q	R	S	T	U	V	W	X	Y	Z
GRADE LEVELS																
Fourth Grade				▨	▨	▨	▨	▨	▨							
Fifth Grade							▨	▨	▨	▨	▨	▨	▨	▨		
Sixth Grade								▨	▨	▨	▨	▨	▨	▨	▨	▨

☐ Approximate grade level

—Based on Pinnell and Fountas, 2001

Make Your Classroom Library the Reliable Source for Leveled Books

The most economical way you can arrive at a significant collection of leveled books is to establish a central collection within the school. This central collection is a place where teachers may go to check out several sets of leveled books for use in the classroom library. Once a teacher has used these books for a reading lesson as planned, the books can be housed temporarily in the classroom library. A central collection is shown in the photograph on the next page.

CHAPTER 4: How Does the Classroom Library Support Reading *With* Children?

83

During independent reading, you will most likely find that students select the books used in guided reading, both to attain greater levels of control and fluency as well as for the sheer pleasure of rereading a familiar book. Children come to realize that their classroom library is the reliable source for these guided reading books and materials. You can make the collection even easier for students to access by establishing shelves expressly allocated for guided reading, as the photograph below illustrates.

Make Your Classroom Library the Reliable Source for an Interesting Variety of Books

In addition to stocking a substantial collection of leveled books, you can create other kinds of classroom library book groupings and materials that provide pivotal support for reading instruction within the reading workshop. For instance, materials for the independent reading or SSR period include personalized reading browsing boxes, magazines, newspapers, and reference materials. You can also use your classroom library to house text sets—sets of different titles, often at varied reading levels, related and grouped by theme, author, or genre.

Text sets can be used in many ways. Multiple titles by the same author enable students to compare and contrast varied examples of a single author's writing (Kotch and Zackman, 1995). Topical collections provide in-depth reading, inquiry, and research experiences for students interested in a specific topic or person. Reading several biographies and historical fiction accounts about, say, Benjamin Franklin can give young readers insights seldom gained from reading a brief textbook section alone. At right and on the next page you'll find two examples of text sets.

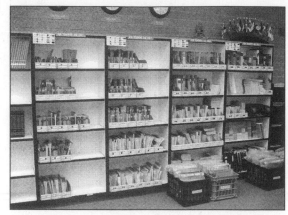

A central collection of leveled books within the school is an economical and efficient way of gathering materials.

Shelves allocated for leveled books help students find what is "just right" for their own reading level.

Author Study
For Younger Readers

William Steig is a master at creating interesting characters and engaging stories—and at choosing just the right words for his descriptions. These books are particularly rich sources for focusing on precise word choice or on the development of fascinating characters:

Amos & Boris

Gorky Rises

Brave Irene

Shrek!

Doctor DeSoto

—Adapted from *Teaching Writing With Picture Books as Models*, Kurstedt and Koutras, 2000, p. 41

Put Books at the Core of Intermediate-Grade Mini-Lessons

Selected mini-lessons are an important part of teaching reading at the intermediate level; they can be held directly within a classroom library. We believe that the best arrangement is to hold reading instruction around a U-shaped or kidney-shaped table with the teacher in the middle of a group of readers. This arrangement allows the teacher to observe, assess, and coach while remaining part of the group.

Reading instruction around a U-shaped table can be held directly in the classroom library.

The right book at the right time can allow a mini-lesson to take off. You can use books to demonstrate, illustrate, and model what authors do in their writing and what readers need to do in order to arrive at real understanding of the text. All the mini-lessons are aimed at helping intermediate-grade learners become independent and critical readers of text. What better way to do this than to use well-chosen books to both lead off and back up your instruction?

There are typically three types of intermediate-level mini-lessons: procedural, skill and strategy, and literary.

Procedural mini-lessons inform students about:

* ❀ Procedures
* ❀ Expectations
* ❀ Assignments
* ❀ Options for responding to reading

CHAPTER 4: How Does the Classroom Library Support Reading *With* Children?

85

Skill and strategy mini-lessons focus on modeling for students how fluent readers use reading stategies such as:

- Predicting
- Inferring
- Visualizing

Literary mini-lessons focus on helping students to:

- Respond to literature
- Understand literary elements such as foreshadowing, flashback, and symbolism
- Use imagery as a tool for comprehension
- Interpret characters' dialogue

The following example of a fifth-grade mini-lesson is based on the book *Sadako and the Thousand Paper Cranes* by Eleanor Coerr. The book is well suited to an interpretation of characters' dialogue because it is a mature story filled with implied meanings and with rich conversations among the main characters.

Sample Mini-Lesson

LESSON: *Exploring Implied Meanings by Interpreting Characters' Dialogue*

Grade: Fifth

Summary of pages 42 and 44

Sadako is in the hospital, ill with radiation sickness, and she meets nine-year-old Kenji for the first time. Kenji tells Sadako that he will die from leukemia soon. Trying to comfort her new friend, Sadako tells Kenji to fold paper cranes "so that a miracle can happen." Nurse Yasunaga overhears Kenji explain to Sadako that it's too late for doctors or miracles to save his life. When the nurse asks Kenji how he can know such things, Kenji replies, "I can read my blood count on the chart. Every day it gets worse."

Quickly, Nurse Yasunaga wheels Kenji out of the room, leaving Sadako to wonder what it would be like to be Kenji—ill and alone in the hospital with no family.

PART I: Interpreting Characters' Dialogue

- Explain that by studying what characters say, it's possible to draw conclusions about their personalities and infer their motivations for actions and decisions. The author doesn't state these meanings; he implies them. Readers are like detectives, discovering the hidden meanings embedded in a character's words.

- Select a rich dialogue between two or three characters. Fifth graders and I reread pages 42-44, the dialogue between Kenji, the nurse, and Sadako. I model how I read between the lines and draw conclusions about Kenji and Sadako: *Kenyi is realistic about his leukemia. He says that he'll die soon. This shows he's accepted death. He backs his statements up by telling Sadako that he reads the blood counts on his chart and they are lower every day. Even the nurse doesn't know what to do with Kenji's honesty—the author says she's "flustered." I felt that way when my father told me that he was going to die. I felt confused and awkward as I tried to refute what I knew in my heart would happen.*

- Ask students to identify the inferences in your think-aloud and what the characters said that made you draw these conclusions.

- Have students point out the personal connection you made. I explain that making personal connections links the character's experiences to my life and can clarify the inference.

❈ Invite students to offer additional thoughts about the character you discussed. A fifth grader points out that Kenji also says that the cranes and even the gods can't help him. He shows courage to Sadako, for Kenji doesn't cry, even though he knows he'll die soon.

❈ Ask students to explain what conclusions they can draw about the other characters in the dialogue. A student focuses on the nurse and says: "She [the nurse] can't handle Kenji's honesty. She asks him how he could know he will die. Then she is caring about Sadako who is also very sick. I know that because the nurse wheels Kenji away so Sadako won't hear anymore."

❈ When I ask, "Why does Sadako deny that Kenji has leukemia and then suggest that Kenji make paper cranes?" another student points out: "She first denies that Kenji has leukemia by saying 'you weren't even born then.' I think she's trying to convince herself that she wasn't born then, either, and can't be that sick. Sadako puts thoughts of her illness aside and tries to comfort Kenji when she suggests he makes cranes. But Sadako has still not connected Kenji's fate to her own, for she wonders what it would be like to be sick like Kenji and have no family."

Prompts That Support Inferring From Dialogue and Inner Thoughts

As you teach students to infer from characters' words, actions, and thoughts, you can scaffold their learning with these prompts:

❈ Why did the character say that [restate the words]?

❈ Why were the inner thoughts different from the spoken words?

❈ Why won't the character say his/her inner thoughts out loud?

❈ Does the situation or setting for the dialogue help you draw conclusions about the character's feelings? thoughts? personality?

❈ Using events that came before these words, explain what motivated the character to speak this way.

❈ How does the tone of voice you imagine for the character help you understand his or her mood? feelings?

❈ Try to visualize the character's expression and gestures. What can you infer from these?

❈ Can you select words the character says that enable you to infer feelings, attitude, personality, inner conflicts?

—From *Teaching Reading in Middle School*, Laura Robb, 2000, pp. 168–169

Put Books at the Core of Intermediate-Grade Literature Response Group Meetings

Literature response group (LRG) meetings, also called literature circles, are a central part of the intermediate-grade reading workshop. Each group meeting lasts about 20 minutes and offers students and teacher a focused opportunity to discuss a particular section of a book. Start off the LRG by presenting a menu of three books to your students during an informal book talk. Students vote for their favorite title. Based on the vote, you then place students into three different LRGs. While you meet with one group of students, the others might read books of their own choosing or read LRG "goal" pages.

In order to guide and shape the discussion during the LRG meeting, a literature response activity—such as "Sketch to Stretch" (Short, Short, Harste, and Burke, 1995; Siegel, 1983)—works well. The activity you choose should permit students to engage in genuine thought or feeling about the selected book. This particular activity offers a wonderful opportunity for students to draw pictures illustrating their favorite part of the story. The steps used in a "Sketch to Stretch" activity are shown at right.

Books that are especially engaging, both humorous and serious, work well for this activity. For younger readers, you might consider any of the Commander Toad books by Jane Yolen or the Berenstein Bear books by Jan and Stan Berenstein. For somewhat older readers, Daniel Pinkwater's books (*The Hoboken Chicken Emergency*, for example) or Bruce Coville's works (*Jennifer Murdley's Toad* or *Aliens Ate My Homework*) are very popular and will almost certainly elicit reactions. One fifth-grade teacher noticed how much her class loved Gail Carson Levine's *Ella Enchanted*. She asked them to envision their favorite episodes and draw large detailed illustrations with captions describing the episodes. The resulting images of ogres, gnomes, and Ella with Prince Char were full of imagination and emotion. This activity helps remind teachers about the power of linking art and literature, something that is often forgotten by the upper grades.

MINI-LESSON: *Sketch to Stretch Activity*

❋ After reading the story, each child independently reflects on his or her favorite part. Then, the children draw their own interpretation of the story. Plenty of time should be given for students to complete their sketches. Remember that the emphasis is on meaning, not artistic ability.

❋ Next, each student shares his or her sketch with the group (without comment) and invites the others to speculate on its meaning as related to the goal pages. Once the questions and comments of the other children are concluded, the artist has the final word.

❋ After each child in the group has shared his or her sketch, the group may wish to pick one sketch to share with the whole class later on. The sketch chosen by the group usually offers a good synopsis of the book or story.

Literature response group activities like "Sketch to Stretch" are aimed at helping students develop a spirit of risk taking as they react to their reading. The best activities help them realize that there is no single correct response and that interpretations depend on a reader's background knowledge and interests. Here is another possible activity:

The Live Interview

When students are involved in guided reading, literature circles or book discussion groups, one thing that elicits a heightened response to characters and plot is the "Live Interview," complete with microphone. You don't even need to have the mike attached to anything. Just holding it in front of a child's face and asking a question brings out the most wonderful response, though you may want to record the lively exchange. At first, you, the teacher, take on the interviewer or news reporter job with a studio audience (the students). You'll say, "Today, folks, we have as our guests the cast of the book *Bud, Not Buddy* by Christopher Paul Curtis (Delacorte, 1999). We're hoping to get to know our characters a little better. First off, is Todd in the audience? Come on up here, Toddy, and tell us about that foster child your parents took in." Selecting a child from the class, the teacher has "Todd" come up to the Interview Chair. "Well, Todd, you and Bud certainly didn't get along the one night he spent in your house. Can you tell us your side of the story?"

And they're off and running. You can interview major and minor characters in the story, or bystanders. Even Bud's late mother can come back from the grave and tell what he was like when he was younger. This allows students to get far deeper into a character than if you simply asked, "What kind of boy was Bud?" and waited for the six usual kids to raise their hands. It's the quietest children who often surprise us the most with this activity. Students can break into small interview groups, write a list of questions that they would ask each character, and then conduct interviews with a moderator and his or her guests.

— Judy Freeman, children's literature consultant, *Book Talk* columnist for *Instructor* magazine, and author of *More Books Kids Will Sit Still For* (Bowker/Greenwood, 1995)

At the conclusion of a particular literature study cycle, you might use your classroom library as this teacher does:

Literature **Study** Display

Books that were previously used as literature study choices are later added to a special spot in the library. These are books the children are familiar with because other reading groups have engaged in book talks and activities about them. These are always high-interest books! Following the completion of a literature study group, I make a point of putting these books into a special display. They are always accompanied by a book review from one of the group members. This display is completely full of books by the end of the year. They are some of the most read books.

— From Jean Turner, fourth-grade teacher, Mt. Loafer Elementary School, Salem, UT

Use Your Classroom Library to Make the Reading-Writing Connection Come Alive

Studying the author's craft is a major focus of instruction for students at the intermediate level. It is at this age that students begin to understand what it means to read like a writer. In other words, students further develop their use of reading strategies and understanding of text by directly experiencing what goes into the writing and structuring of text from the writer's point of view. And the greater their exposure to different types of writing, the broader will become their understanding of the many ways in which writing can express one's feelings and needs. Thus, writing instruction and dedicated writing time complement the reading workshop framework to integrate reading with writing.

Almost any written materials—joke and riddle collections, poetry, greeting cards, cookbooks, guidebooks, brochures, play scripts, e-mails, and diaries, along with novels and nonfiction books—are fair game. With its stock of many different kinds of sources and its varied titles (see Chapter 1 for a full listing), your classroom library is a natural home for your focus on the reading-writing connection. It not only houses examples of various books and materials written by published authors, but it also provides displays of how to write in these various genres.

Getting to know something about the people behind the books is motivating for young writers, and the classroom library is the ideal spot to invite students to engage in studying authors. You can set up a section of the classroom library dedicated to displaying information about particular authors. Because a number of authors even encourage students to communicate with them through letters and e-mail, addresses and contact information can also be provided in the classroom library.

You can also give student writing projects— once in final form and "published"—a prominent place in the classroom library. Place stick-on pockets and library cards in the back of student-authored books and then catalogue and place these books in the classroom library for other students to read. Displaying them with their covers facing out will allow the student author to feel even greater pride and will make it easier for other students to find these books. In our experiences, these child-authored books often became class favorites!

Student-authored books, displayed in the classroom library, are usually very popular reading choices.

Writer's Craft Mini-Lessons

Writer's craft mini-lessons are an important part of overall writing instruction at this level. Mini-lessons accomplish the following:

1. Equip students with necessary skills and strategies for writing a variety of text compositions.

2. Teach students how to employ a variety of literary techniques.

3. Provide students with an understanding of the many tools authors use.

One of the best ways to demonstrate a particular literary technique or text structure is to select a book or a cluster of books strong in that element and incorporate these into the heart of your lesson. This means that the classroom library can be a wonderful resource and ideal location for writing instruction mini-lessons. Below you'll find a list of possible writers' craft lesson ideas. Following that is a sample mini-lesson that puts library books at the core of instruction.

Sample Mini-Lesson

LESSON: *Voice and Point of View*

After we've introduced mood, we discuss voice and point of view, talking about how they can contribute to mood. We try changing the voice and point of view of a piece and notice the effect that has on the story. A few of the lessons we teach to help students understand and use voice and point of view follow.

Voice

A book we like to use to launch our discussion of voice is *Tight Times* by Barbara Shook Hazen. It's a poignant story about a young boy whose parents won't let him get a dog because of financial hardship. In large part, the poignancy is due to the boy's voice that comes through so vividly in the story. He cannot understand why he can't have a dog. The explanation of "tight times" is meaningless to him, so he takes matters into his own hands by adopting a cat.

Book Excerpt: *Tight Times*

> I tiptoed into the kitchen. I tried to be quiet. But the milk was up too high. It tipped and made a terrible mess. Mommy and Daddy ran out of their rooms. Daddy looked funny. He looked at the cat. Then he looked at me. "What is that!" he asked. "It's a cat," I told him. "A nice lady said I could keep it. And I didn't go near the street." Then something sort of scary happened. Daddy started to cry. So did Mommy. I didn't know daddies cried. I didn't know what to do. Then they both made a sandwich hug with me in the middle. So I started to cry.

The boy's voice comes through in the short sentences he uses to narrate this incident and in the way he interprets the events. His parents are moved because the boy's desire for a pet was so strong that it led him to bend their rules, although we can tell he's usually conscientious about keeping them: He didn't go near the street; he tried not to disturb his parents; he's concerned about making a mess. He doesn't know what to make of their show of emotion, so he resorts to crying himself. The word choice, sentence length, and dialogue help the young boy's voice shine through.

Choosing an appropriate voice for a piece depends on the narrator—who is speaking—and the audience—who is being addressed. For

CHAPTER 4: How Does the Classroom Library Support Reading *With* Children?

⟨ 91 ⟩

memoirs, the speaker is the student; we help students bring their own voice to their pieces by suggesting they pretend they're speaking to a friend. For nonfiction—for example, an editorial—the voice is still the student's, but thinking of the intended audience becomes important when deciding how to express that voice. We often encourage students to talk into a tape recorder or to a partner the way they'd like to sound addressing their audience; then they can play it back and try to capture that voice in their writing. For fiction, when students usually adopt the voice of a character, their knowledge of the character helps them choose which of the strategies we've discussed will best bring out the strong and unique voice of that character.

Point of View

It's difficult, if not impossible, to separate voice and point of view, as evidenced by the above example. Our discussion of voice in *Tight Times* naturally leads us to point of view. One reason we like to use this book is that it provides the perspective of the father juxtaposed with that of the son. Take a look at this excerpt from the book, in which the father is trying to explain "tight times" to his son.

Book Excerpt: *Tight Times*

He said tight times are when everything keeps going up.

I had a balloon that did that once.

Daddy said tight times are why we all eat Mr. Bulk instead of cereals in little boxes.

I like little boxes better.

Daddy said tight times are why we went to the sprinkler last summer instead of the lake.

I like the lake better.

Daddy said tight times are why we don't have a roast beef on Sunday.

Instead we have soupy things with lima beans.
I hate lima beans.

If I had a dog, I'd make him eat mine.

Each of the father's explanations is followed by the child's response. The gulf of understanding between the two is highlighted by this rhetorical structure, which serves as a wonderful jumping-off point for a discussion of point of view. We encourage students to be aware of the words they choose when writing and provide them with plenty of picture book models of effective use of voice and point of view.

Two Characters, Two Stories, One Plot

Another good book for exploring point of view is *The Pain and the Great One* by Judy Blume. The book is divided into two parts, "The Pain" and "The Great One." Each part is told from the point of view of one of the characters and thus has its own distinct voice.

As you can imagine, although the situation is the same, the stories are quite different, thus providing our students with another clear example of how voice and point of view can play a major role in shaping a piece of writing.

Point of view and voice are difficult concepts for young writers to apply to their own writing. To help them choose a perspective and voice for their stories and reports, we present them with the following guidelines.

❀ Think about the event, issue, or topic you're planning to write about.

❀ From whose point of view do you want to write? Whose point of view seems natural to you?

❀ Once you've decided on a point of view, remember to stick with it throughout your piece!

❀ Now think about the voice you want to use to convey your ideas.

—From *Teaching Writing with Picture Books as Models,* Rosanne Kurstedt and Maria Koutras, 2000, pp. 64–66

Use Your Classroom Library to Reinforce Reading and Language Instruction

Your regular reading instruction will not always be sufficient for all students to maintain their progress in reading. Sometimes intensive, focused mini-lessons are called for; they help refine and develop students' use of strategies in order to meet the challenges of more difficult words and books. They also help students understand authors' uses of more interesting and sophisticated literary elements. These additional mini-lessons can be taught to the whole class, in needs groups, or with individual students to help sustain reading progress and expand upon students' repertoire of strategies for constructing meaning.

Strategies for sustaining students' progress in reading include:

1. Solving words
2. Finding the important information
3. Predicting
4. Maintaining fluency
2. Monitoring and correcting
2. Adjusting

Strategies for expanding students' reading comprehension include:

1. Connecting
2. Inferring
3. Summarizing
4. Synthesizing
5. Analyzing
6. Evaluating

By the time students are well into the intermediate years, they often use these interrelated sets of sustaining strategies automatically. But during the intermediate years there is an important phase in reading instruction when the teacher needs to give students demonstrations about how, when, and why any of these various strategies are selected and applied.

Below we look at how the classroom library can support your instruction of three of these strategies.

Word Solving

The classroom library is an ideal location to:

❉ Store letter and word manipulatives, such as magnetic letters, letter and word part cards, word cards for making compound words, counting chips for counting sounds, prefix and suffix cards, and Latin and Greek root cards.

CHAPTER 4: How Does the Classroom Library Support Reading *With* Children?

❮ 93 ❯

* Provide a small table for students to work in pairs or small groups to make and sort words.

* House multiple copies of the dictionary, thesaurus, and other word-list books for students to study and learn about words and word families.

* Offer a display area for lists of prefixes, suffixes, Greek and Latin roots, and student-made words.

* Hold mini-lessons focused on word solving and on developing word meanings. These mini-lessons can make use of specific word-oriented books that will help you demonstrate the point of the lesson. For instance, *Sniglets* by R. Hal is a wonderful book that is full of fun words that aren't in the dictionary but should be! A few other books that work well for word play and word learning are *The Weighty Word Book* (Leavit Stevens, Burger, and Guralnik) and *The Pig in the Spigot* or *The Disappearing Alphabet* (both by Richard Wilbur).

Mini-lessons to help students with word solving may include topics found below:

Word Solving Mini-Lessons

* Making words that start or end in the same way

* Making words that contain silent letters

* Making words into contractions

* Making compound words

* Making words using prefixes and suffixes

* Making words that sound the same but are spelled differently

* Making words using Latin or Greek roots

* Making words that use a common rhyme or word family part, such as *ick, an, un,* or *ast.*

* Counting sounds to make simple one-syllable words.

* Making words that have the same number of syllables

* Sorting words into categories children can discover (open sorts) or into teacher-directed/predetermined categories (closed sorts) using sounds, spelling, or meaning as the basis for sorting

* Making word meaning webs or semantic maps to organize words around meaning categories such as tools, colors, actions, and so forth

Finding the Important Information

Effective reading involves separating the important information from the less important details. Helping children develop the ability to do this involves modeling for them what you do and how you do it as a reader. For instance, you can ask students to read a text with you and make a list of the important information. Also, in introducing students to a new text during a reading lesson, you can point out the important information to help them focus their attention on what is key.

In the classroom library, you might set aside a small collection of books containing text that lends itself to the sifting of important from unimportant information. For example, E. Little's *The Trojan Horse: How the Greeks Won the War* provides an opportunity for students to sort out the important aspects of winning a war from inconsequential details. You should mark portions of a book like this ahead of time to demonstrate the two categories. Have students sit at a table and sort sentence strips taken from the book into piles labeled "important" and "unimportant." A self-correcting key can be used to check and discuss the results of the students' sorting activity.

Making Predictions

As children read, they combine language on the page with their own knowledge to help them predict what may come next. Making predictions is not only a key comprehension skill, it also helps readers figure out new words. Share books with children that invite both predictions and word solving. A favorite book for this purpose is James Howe's *Bunnicula*, the tale of a vampire bunny who sucks vegetable juice out of carrots. As preparation for reading this book, you may want to discuss the topic of vampires with students. Then, as they read the text, ask them to watch for any clues that this bunny is no regular bunny.

You might also use the classroom library to house a small collection of Nate the Great (Sharmat) or Encyclopedia Brown (Sobal) series books; this might be especially effective in a mystery center where predictions are displayed. You could place a "mystery box" in this center for students' predictions. Another box, the "mystery solved box," could also be placed here for students to share the mystery solutions after reading the books. Other excellent books to use for modeling how to make predictions are *White Wash* by Ntzoake Shange; *Zeke Peppin* by William Steig; *The Lily Cupboard* by Shulamith Levey Oppenheim; and *Peppe, the Lamplighter* by Eliza Bartone.

CHAPTER 5

How Does the Classroom Library Support Reading *by* Children?

Scenario 1: Word spread rapidly among students in Mrs. Salcido's fifth-grade class. The new Harry Potter book, *Harry Potter and the Goblet of Fire* (Rowling, 2000), would be arriving in the school library tomorrow. Many of the students had already read the first three books in the series and there was much discussion about the next episode. The preceding books had been the focus of conversation among students in class, at recess, in the school library, and, in many cases, even at home. Now, the only question was how many copies the school library would get in. Clearly, there were many more students who wanted to read this book than there would be available copies. Then, one of the students reminded everyone that because they had just gone to the school library yesterday, their class was not scheduled to visit for two more weeks. The high level of excitement subsided as the students realized the book would already be checked out before they returned to the library.

Scenario 2: Ms. Thomas had just completed *The Summer of the Monkeys* (Rawls, 1976) as a class Read Aloud. Her experience had taught her that students often wanted to revisit stories they had listened to, so she had made sure that there were several copies of the book in the classroom library. She had also made a list of related books that children in her fifth-grade class might be interested in reading independently. When students were invited to visit the classroom library to select a book for voluntary reading, many had already made a mental note, from their teacher's suggestions, of several books they might choose. Ms. Thomas knew how critical it was for students in this grade level to experience a wide range of reading genres to enhance their ability to make successful book selections. Therefore, her class Read Aloud selections represented a wide range of genres. Also aware of the critical importance that access to material plays in maintaining students' interest in reading, she always made sure that there were extra copies of her Read Aloud books in the classroom library.

These scenarios represent two very different approaches by teachers to support their students' interest in independent reading. Mrs. Salcido does not take advantage of her students' high level of interest in a particular text. When her students realize that their access to the book will be delayed, they express frustration that may eventually be translated into a general lack of interest in reading. On the other hand, Ms. Thomas recognizes that her students must have ready access to a wide range of reading material within the classroom. She not only makes sure the Read Aloud book is available in the classroom library, but she also stocks the library so that students will have access to related books in the immediate future.

It is now well accepted that access to a wide range of reading material in the home influences a child's success in learning to read (Neuman, 1999; Clark, 1976; Durkin, 1966; Tobin, 1981). These children experience a greater likelihood of being successful readers than those who do not have access. It is not any less important to provide this same support for children as they expand their reading experience in school. As we will explore in this chapter, a well thought-out classroom library strengthens a teacher's ability to encourage children to read independently.

Why It Is Important for Students to Participate in Voluntary Reading

In addition to overwhelming agreement among parents, educators, and others that independent reading results in increased and improved reading, empirical research indicates a strong correlation between independent or voluntary reading and reading achievement (Anderson, Wilson, and Fielding, 1988; Morrow, 1985). Children engaged in voluntary reading through the middle grades generally attain higher levels of achievement in reading comprehension and vocabulary. While time spent reading was one of the factors measured in these studies, additional research points out the important role discussion plays in helping children to develop sophisticated language, broader background knowledge, and an understanding of how stories are put together (Brown and Cambourne, 1987; Gambrell and Almasi, 1996). Thus, research supports what intuition and anecdotal evidence tell us: the more students engage in voluntary reading and have opportunities to discuss their reading with others, the greater reading achievement, interest, and motivation they will experience toward reading.

Students with a negative attitude toward reading generally view it simply as a "school activity" and not something they would choose to do for recreation or pleasure or to learn new things on their own (Worthy, 1996). In-school reading is often characterized by little time for self-selection of material; limited opportunities for discussion around books; and mundane tasks that have little relevance to the interests of the students. However, when they are read to, or when they can read about topics that are of interest to them, these same students acknowledge that in-school reading activities can bring pleasure.

In most classrooms, the opportunity for student book choice based on interest occurs far too infrequently. Many teachers allow independent reading only when students have completed other instructional tasks, such as worksheet or workbook activities, and few regularly schedule independent reading time. However, such opportunities can greatly increase motivation and achievement. We strongly suggest that you regularly set aside time for both independent reading and book discussion.

You can make independent reading fun for your students by showing your own excitement about it. Here are several ideas for motivating your students to care about independent reading and about making their own book choices.

Regularly scheduled independent reading time increases motivation to read.

Use Books to Get Students Excited about Reading

❈ **Great Books Plus Modeling = Insatiable Readers:** Step one in getting children excited about reading books is modeling. You are the reading role model for your students. The way you read aloud or give a book talk (a book "commercial" where you tell just enough about the plot to tantalize your listeners) is what gets your class revved up to do the same. In addition to the longer chapter books you read aloud to your children on a daily basis, it is easy to introduce them to dozens more books every week. Select a range of five irresistible books a day, for which you present quick one-sentence book talks and Read Alouds of pertinent chapters, pages, paragraphs, or even one-sentence memorable lines. Then hand the books out to the children, who will have their appetites whetted by now. Don't be surprised if they throng around you and clamor, "May I have that one!" Or raffle the books off with great fanfare, saying, "If you can guess the number (or color or state or city) that's in my head right now, this book is yours to read!"*

❈ **Laughing Day:** You can also have your students model and share their favorites with the rest of the group. For instance, start by doing a book talk and reading aloud passages from "books that make you fall off your bed laughing." Then tell your students that next week you want them to each find and read a book from the classroom library that makes them laugh out loud. They should pick a passage of no more than half a page to read aloud to the whole class. Remind them to include something that will show the class just how funny the book really is. On a specially designated "Laughing Day," push all the desks together or make a large circle of chairs. Within this readers' roundtable, you will all be able to see each other, King Arthur-style, and to connect via humor. And before you know it, students will be seeking out their friends' recommendations in the classroom library.*

❈ **Desert Island Books:** One of my favorite book talks is "Books to Take to a Desert Island." After describing to my fifth-grade class the books I'd want with me if I were marooned on an island, I give them an assignment: They have one week to pick their favorite book, develop a 30-second book talk about it, and plan to dress for the occasion. I decorate our readers' roundtable with island-related things—seashells, plants, buckets, a blanket, and even a big beach umbrella. The children have great fun showing up in sandals, sunglasses, and straw hats. In one class, a girl wore an old grass skirt over her jeans; it shed all day until the entire floor was covered with it and all she had left was the waistband. We always have a wonderful, tropical time celebrating books on "Desert Island' Day."*

❈ **The "What's New" Shelf:** When new books arrive in our classroom (from book orders or my own shopping), I do a quick "book sell" by briefly introducing the books and then placing them on a special "What's New" shelf. This shelf holds a prominent place of honor in our classroom library. I often introduce themed book baskets in this way as well. Doing this increases student interest and curiosity and encourages students to try something new.**

* Judy Freeman, children's literature consultant, *Book Talk* columnist for *Instructor* magazine, and author of *More Books Kids Will Sit Still For* (Bowker/Greenwood, 1995)

** Diane Miness, first-grade teacher, Dutch Neck School, Princeton Junction, NJ

Celebrating books on "Desert Island Day."

How Motivation for Voluntary Reading Is Influenced by Ready Access to Books

More than 30 years ago, Bissett (1969) discovered that children who had ready access to literature in their classrooms read 50 percent more than children in classrooms without literature. Research in reading over the past decade has continued to address the role of motivation and interest in reading. Several researchers in particular (Turner and Paris, 1995; Gambrell, 1996) have conducted research to assess which classroom characteristics seem to influence students' desire to become active readers. The characteristics that have emerged are summarized below.

Based on this research and our own experience, we believe that ready access to a large number of diverse kinds of books is a key starting point for a motivated reader.

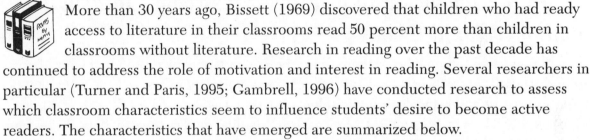

Factors Affecting Motivation to Read

❖ Student choice of reading material and follow-up activities

❖ Student control over learning experiences

❖ Access to a wide range of reading materials in the classroom

❖ Opportunities for students to share information about their reading with others

❖ Peer recommendations of and social interaction around books

❖ Teachers who serve as models through Read Alouds, shared reading, guided reading, and their own independent reading

❖ Positive consequences for reading

❖ Opportunities to share successes and failures with reading

❖ Appropriate literacy incentives, such as books, magazines, pencils, pens, markers, writing pads, and letter stencils

Chapter 5: How Does the Classroom Library Support Reading *by* Children?

101

The Role of the Classroom Library in Motivating and Supporting Voluntary Reading

 As we discussed in Chapter 1, the specific attributes of an effective classroom library include sufficient space; comfortable seating; the feeling of privacy and peace; literature displays and posters; shelving that permits easy student browsing; and many different genres and reading levels represented. You may want to look back to Chapter 1 for a fuller description of these and other criteria. Unless the classroom library is set up in this manner, the chances of its being used as a strong support for independent reading will be limited. A well-designed classroom library capitalizes on what we know about motivating student reading.

Access to a wide range of reading materials encourages independent reading.

Focus on One Factor in an Effective Classroom Library: The Element of Student Choice

We will focus here on one factor to make our point: student choice. Building your library around student interests can draw in even reluctant readers. For instance, Worthy (1996) spent some time following sixth-grade reluctant readers as they visited the school library. Through interviews, she found that their favorite reading materials were scary stories and novels, cartoon books, sports materials (including magazines), drawing books, series books, and popular magazines. Specifically stocking the classroom library with these kinds of materials would be a natural step in addressing these readers' interests and needs and in whetting their appetites as burgeoning readers.

In the scenario on the next page, both teachers are interested in the same goal—helping students become avid, independent readers—but only one of the teachers makes full use of the classroom library and manages to achieve this goal.

Determine Students Interests

So how do you discover and determine your students' interests in order to go about setting up a successful classroom library that will best support independent reading? There are several means we recommend.

Interviews and Inventories

One relatively simple method is interviewing. A framework for the interview is very helpful; you can construct your own framework quite easily, or you might use one of those

TEACHING IN ACTION: *Two Teachers—Same Goal but Very Different Results*

Mr. Prichett is a fifth-grade teacher who wants his students to enjoy reading. He tries to read quality chapter books to the children each day. He makes sure that his students have access to the school library each week without fail. His school's principal has let all the teachers know that students should have opportunities for reading independently each day. As a result, Mr. Prichett's students begin each school day with sustained silent reading (SSR). However, in all honesty, Mr. Prichett does not always feel this is the best use of time since many of his students do not actually read during SSR. He is constantly reminding them to come to class prepared with a book to read and that once SSR time begins, all students should be quiet and begin reading their books. While he knows that independent reading is important, he hasn't found a way to engage students in voluntary reading that doesn't require constant prodding. He has become frustrated and so have his students.

Miss Todachinnie, on the other hand, is having great success engaging her students in reading. At the beginning of the year, she had each of her students respond to an interest inventory about reading. Through this, she noticed that her students were interested in a wide range of text, including newspapers, magazines, comic books, picture books, and chapter books. She knows that visiting the school library once

a week will not sustain student interest in reading for very long, so she has been working on expanding her classroom collection over the previous few years. She now has a fairly sizable collection of books (around 350) in the room for her students to access. However, from her students' responses to the interest inventory, she realizes that she needs to provide an even wider range of choices. She begins to collect comic books and magazines that she thinks are appropriate for her students to read and will meet parent expectations for their children. She also finds that the local newspaper is willing to donate several copies of the paper each day to her school. This provides new material for her library each week that encourages student excitement.

Miss Todachinnie makes it a point to include student-written books in her classroom library. This seems to really encourage her students to want to write during writing time. She also implements an instructional routine that provides longer blocks of time for students to be in the classroom library for independent reading multiple times throughout the day. She allots time for students to share what they are reading. As the year progresses, she has to make minor modifications in her routine but she is very pleased with the interest students are demonstrating in reading on their own.

presented below. Use them as the basis for an individual oral interview, or distribute them to the class for written responses.

The first is a reading interest inventory, which is targeted specifically to reading materials. The second is a more general set of questions. Each can provide you with invaluable insights into your students' concerns, interests, and needs.

READING INTEREST INVENTORY
(Sample 1)

	Often		Sometimes		Not at all
1. I like to read about people who have real problems.	5	4	3	2	1
2. I like stories about finding clues and solving mysteries.	5	4	3	2	1
3. I like to read poetry.	5	4	3	2	1
4. I like books with many pictures.	5	4	3	2	1
5. I like stories about people in love.	5	4	3	2	1
6. I like legends and tall tales.	5	4	3	2	1
7. I like funny stories.	5	4	3	2	1
8. I like books about animals.	5	4	3	2	1
9. I like make-believe stories about traveling in space.	5	4	3	2	1
10. I like books about important people.	5	4	3	2	1
11. I like sports stories.	5	4	3	2	1
12. I like to read plays.	5	4	3	2	1
13. I like science books.	5	4	3	2	1
14. I like stories about people from long ago.	5	4	3	2	1
15. I like adventure stories that take place outdoors.	5	4	3	2	1
16. I like stories about imaginary animals and creatures and things that couldn't possibly happen.	5	4	3	2	1
17. I like reading stories that use cartoon characters.	5	4	3	2	1
18. I like reading popular magazines.	5	4	3	2	1
19. I like reading the newspaper.	5	4	3	2	1

READING INTEREST INVENTORY
(Sample 2)

Student Name: _____

Answer each of the following questions.

1. What do you like to do in your free time?

   _____

2 Would you rather go to a sporting event or the zoo?

   _____

3. Would you rather go to a bookstore or a music store?

   _____

4. Would you rather write about an imaginary being or about scientific discoveries made by astronauts?

   _____

5. Which TV show do you like to watch the most?

   _____

6. When you are with your friends, what do you like to do the most?

   _____

7. Which activities or hobbies are you really good at?

   _____

Reading Genre Wheels

Sometimes, students will not be able to identify their interests. In these cases you should give them an opportunity to read material from a wide range of genres. You can use a reading genre wheel, such as the one illustrated here, to aid students in discovering the many options they have in reading material.

We encourage students to color in each "piece of the pie" when they have read a book from the genre represented. They shouldn't read another book from that genre until they have colored in the whole wheel. Many times students will be exposed via this experience to different types of text that they have not encountered yet in their reading; they

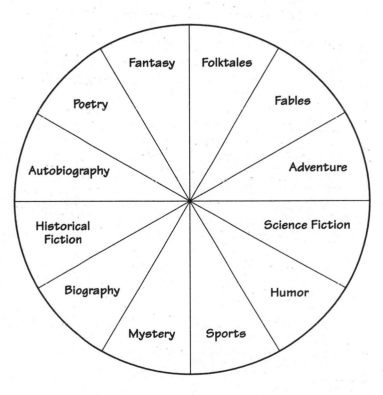

Chapter 5: How Does the Classroom Library Support Reading *by* Children?

{ 105 }

come away with their attention captured by new kinds of books.

In addition to providing each student with his or her own copy of this diagram, you might want to make a poster-sized version to mount in your classroom library. As a poster it could be used in several different ways: It might be colored in like a graph to demonstrate overall class preferences or it might include write-on lines for students to jot in titles they have read.

Diverse books representing all genres and a comfortable reading nook are a great start for a classroom library.

Include Books That Represent All Genres

In order for the genre wheel activity to be successful, it is essential to have numerous texts on hand so that the various categories in the genre wheel are all available to students as they make their selections. Afterward, of course, you need to continue to make books from all genres available to sustain and support the choices students have made. For these reasons, we provide a listing of books organized by genre for all the categories in the genre wheel. The list is meant to complement those in Chapters 1 and 4 and as with those, we remind you that the titles here represent only a small sampling of the many excellent children's literature books now available.

Suggested Book Titles for the Genre Wheel

FABLES

Primary	Intermediate
Aesop's Fables (Hague)	*Misoso: Once Upon a Time Tales from Africa* (Aardema)
Aesop's Fables (Holder)	*Aesop's Fables* (Kredel)

ADVENTURE

Primary	Intermediate
Elephants Aloft (Baker)	*The Voyage of the Frog* (Paulsen)
The Steadfast Tin Soldier (Lynch)	*The Cay* (Taylor)
Danger Guys on Ice (Abbott)	

SCIENCE FICTION

Primary	Intermediate
Jed's Junior Space Patrol (Marzollo)	*The Giver* (Lowry)
Commander Toad in Space (Yolen)	*A Wrinkle in Time* (L'Engle)

HUMOR

Primary	Intermediate
George and Martha (Marshall)	*Skinnybones* (Park)
The Stupids Die (Allard)	*Mr. Popper's Penguins* (Atwater)
	How to Eat Fried Worms (Rockwell)

SPORTS

Primary	Intermediate
Never Fear, Flip the Dip is Here (Hanft)	*Athletic Shorts* (Crutcher)
Baseball, Football, Daddy, and Me (Friend)	*Fighting Tackle* (Christopher)
Soccer Game! (Maccarone)	*Face-Off* (Christopher)

MYSTERY

Primary	Intermediate
Meg Mackintosh and the Case of the Missing Babe Ruth Baseball (Landon)	*The Case of the Baker Street Irregular* (Newman)
Cam Jansen and the Mystery at the Haunted House (Adler)	*The Wolves of Willoughby Chase* (Aiken)
	Encyclopedia Brown: Boy Detective (Sobol)

BIOGRAPHY

Primary	Intermediate
What's the Big Idea, Ben Franklin? (Fritz)	*Joe DiMaggio* (Appel)
A Picture Book of Sitting Bull (Adler)	*As Long as the Rivers Flow* (Allen and Smith)
Thomas Alva Edison: Great Inventor (Adler)	

HISTORICAL FICTION

Primary	Intermediate
Thy Friend Obadiah (Turkle)	*Roll of Thunder, Hear My Cry* (Taylor)
When Jessie Came Across the Sea (Hest and Lynch)	*The Door in the Wall* (De Angeli)

AUTOBIOGRAPHY

Primary	Intermediate
The Art of Eric Carle (Carle)	*In My Own Time: Almost an Autobiography* (Bawden)
Hau Kola = Hello Friend (Goble)	*On the Bus with Joanna Cole* (Saul)
Spyglass: An Autobiography (Deschamps)	

POETRY

Primary	Intermediate
Street Music: City Poems (Adoff)	*Just People and Other Poems for Young Readers* (Appelt)
The Palm of My Heart (Adedjouma)	*Slow Dance Heart Break Blues* (Adoff)
The New Kid on the Block (Prelutsky)	*If I Were in Charge of the World and Other Worries* (Viorst)

FANTASY

Primary

Dmitri the Astronaut (Agee)

In the Night Kitchen (Sendak)

Dinosaur Bob and His Adventures With the

Family Lizardo (Joyce)

My Father's Dragon (Gannett)

Intermediate

Mrs. Frisby and the Rats of NIMH (O'Brien)

The High King (Alexander)

The Indian in the Cupboard (Banks)

Harry Potter and the Sorcerer's Stone (Rowling)

FOLK TALES

Primary

Anansi Does the Impossible (Aardema)

Smokey Mountain Rose: An Appalachian

Cinderella (Schroeder)

Intermediate

The Golden Carp and Other Tales from Vietnam (Vuong)

True Lies: 18 Tales for You to Judge (Shannon)

The Arabian Nights (Philip)

To help students further navigate their way among the different genres and book titles in the classroom library, consider using the following activities:

Helping Students Make Choices

❖ **Reading Territories:** "Reading territories" is an appealing idea that Nancy Atwell suggests. I do a version of this in my own classroom. Students have a territory sheet in which they record the different territories they have been as readers. They log genres and favorites (authors, stories, poems, picture books, rereads, and so on). This activity structures their choices and helps them organize which types of reading they have done and which they still plan to do. I model my own territory log regularly for students. Watching me log my entries always elicits "oohs and aahs" from the students and exclamations of, "You read a lot!" or "You read so many authors!" This activity has been a consistent success for me over the years. It is a real teaching tool as well as a reflective reading organizer, and it has assisted students with developing breadth as well as depth as readers.

❖ **Keeping Up the Suspense and Building Knowledge at the Same Time:** My classroom library is organized in tubs, and each tub is labeled by genre. Although knowledge of genres is important in fourth grade, I have discovered that very often students do not recognize the labels nor understand what the genres mean. So to begin the year, I tape off all the tubs but one. I introduce this genre in a mini-lesson and for a time allow the students to choose only from that tub for independent reading. As the weeks progress, I untape the genre tubs one by one until the students are familiar with each type and with how the library is organized.

— Jean Turner, fourth-grade teacher, Mt Loafer Elementary School, Salem, UT

Genre tubs can be unveiled one by one, as each genre is introduced.

Include Books That Represent Cultural and Ethnic Diversity

You've probably noticed that a number of the titles in the genre book list and in the lists in Chapter 1 and 4 represent diverse cultures. Including multicultural books in your classroom library is another fundamental means of addressing students' needs and interests. Offering children books that are culturally sensitive will not only support improved reading proficiency, but will also help them to gain a greater awareness of themselves and those around them. Because this is such an important goal for your students as readers and such a key criterion for the book selections you make for your classroom library, we provide here a framework for choosing multicultural materials and two lists of specific book titles.

What to Look for in Selecting Multicultural Texts

❖ Books should celebrate diversity and the commonalities across cultures,

❖ The text should support reading development by possessing features such as rhyme, rhythm, repetitive sentences or phrases, cumulative events, and familiar sequences,

❖ All of the books need to be authentic (e.g., genuinely authored and not artificially contrived) texts,

❖ They should be easy to read independently,

❖ The text should be appropriate for the intended age group.

—From Opitz, M.F. 1999

The following table suggests several books and identifies to what degree they meet the criteria.

SUPPORTIVE BOOK CHARACTERISTICS

Title	Date Published	Rhyme/ Rhythm	Repet- ition	Cumulative Events	Familiar Events/ Sequence	Supportive Pictures *	Spanish/ English
Action Alphabet	1996				X	X	
America: My Land, Your Land, Our Land	1997	X	X			X	
Coconut Mon	1995		X		X	X	
Cumbayah	1998	X	X			X	
Feast for 10	1993	X	X		X	X	
Fiesta!	1996		X		X	X	X
Greetings, Sun	1998	X	X		X	X	
Hands!	1997		X		X	X	
I Am Me!	1996				X	X	
My Five Senses	1998		X		X	X	
Navajo ABC	1995				X	X	
No Mirrors in My Nana's House	1998	X	X			X	
Now I'm Big	1996		X		X	X	
Play	1998				X	X	
Somewhere Today	1998		X		X	X	
Tortillas and Lullabies	1998		X		X	X	X
Uno, Dos, Tres; One, Two, Three	1996	X	X		X	X	X
When I First Came to This Land	1998	X	X	X		X	
Whoever You Are	1997		X			X	
Whose Hat?	1997		X			X	
Work	1998				X	X	

* This criteria applies to Hispanic-American culture. Similar criteria may also relate to other cultures influenced by native language.

—From Opitz, 1999

We also recommend the following list of things to look for as you make decisions about which books to select for your classroom library that best represent cultural and ethnic diversity (Pang, Colvin, Tran, and Barba, 1992). These books should include:

- ❀ a theme supportive of cultural pluralism
- ❀ characters that are portrayed in a positive way
- ❀ a story set in the United States

- ❀ illustrations that are genuine
- ❀ a story that presents strong characters with a compelling plot
- ❀ a story that is historically accurate

These researchers applied their criteria to Asian-American children's literature and they recommend the following titles:

RECOMMENDED ASIAN-AMERICAN LITERATURE FOR CHILDREN

TITLE	AUTHOR
A Is for Aloha	Feeney
The Best Bad Thing	Uchida
Child of the Owl	Yep
Children of the River	Crew
Dragonwings	Yep
First Snow	Coutant
The Happiest Ending	Uchida
The Invisible Thread	Uchida
A Jar of Dreams	Uchida
Journey Home	Uchida
The Journey: Japanese Americans, Racism, and Renewal	Hamanaka
Journey to Topaz	Uchida
The Lost Garden: A Memoir	Yep
A River Dream	Say
Samurai of Gold Hill	Uchida
Sea Glass	Yep
The Star Fisher	Yep
Umbrella	Yashima
Wingman	Pinkwater

— Pang, Colvin, Tran, and Barba (1992).

Chapter 5: How Does the Classroom Library Support Reading *by* Children?

❨111❩

Integrate the Classroom Library and Instruction That Supports Independent Reading

Many schools provide opportunities in the daily schedule for children to read stories independently. This period of time goes by different labels in various schools, including DEAR (drop everything and read), USSR (uninterrupted sustained silent reading), and RIS (reading in silence). However, most commonly, this sponsored independent reading time is referred to as SSR (sustained silent reading). In Chapter 4, we mentioned that SSR is a component of the reading workshop. You can incorporate it into your classroom both within that context and on its own as a discrete experience.

When students participate in SSR, they gain significant benefits in reading comprehension and engagement. These benefits are at least as noteworthy as those obtained through skills instruction in reading. Additionally, when you permit children to read books for pleasure during SSR, the students often feel that they have been asked to do less work than during a traditional skill lesson (Pilgreen, 2000).

In using SSR, one of the challenges you will probably experience is how to encourage students to fully participate in this opportunity for independent reading without wasting time. Often, teachers believe it is inappropriate for them to intervene with children who are not engaged in reading during SSR time, fearing that they may distract other children in the class who are reading. However, a small amount of intervention can go a long way toward encouraging less motivated readers. On the following page, we present a mini-lesson aimed at addressing the needs of less motivated readers.

Sample Mini-Lesson

LESSON: Using the Classroom Library to Help Less Motivated Students Become Engaged During SSR

Purpose: To provide support for students who are not engaging in reading during SSR time.

Necessary Supplies/Materials: A completed interest inventory for the identified child; a well-stocked classroom library.

Instructing and Modeling:

* Identify students who habitually are not reading during SSR time.

* Conduct an interest inventory with each student to establish types of reading material he or she is interested in.

* Invite the student to meet with you for a few minutes once the SSR time has begun for the day and the rest of the students are reading their books.

* As you begin the conference with the student, you may choose to ask about the following issues. (Remember that these are only suggested prompts. Other relevant questions are certainly appropriate.)

    What kind of books do you like to read?

    How do you feel about the book you have been reading during SSR? Is it too easy, too difficult, or just right?

Describe for me what you are reading today.

Have you had experiences similar to the characters in the book?

Who was your favorite character?

What new information did you learn from your reading material?

What do you think will happen to the character in your book as you read tomorrow?

* Once you have established the types of books that interest the student, take him or her with you to the classroom library and help select an appropriate book or other material for independent reading.

* Continue to briefly discuss the student's choice of reading material each day for about one week. If the student isn't becoming engaged in the reading, help him or her to make another selection based on the information you now have about interests and motivation.

Monitoring Success: Pay close attention to the student over a period of several weeks and provide support as needed.

Chapter 5: How Does the Classroom Library Support Reading *by* Children?

113

Closing Reflections

Several years ago, as we worked with teachers whose classrooms were otherwise excellent, we noticed that the libraries in these rooms appeared to be afterthoughts. Often haphazard collections of garage-sale and donated books, these single-shelf collections were at best add-ons to classroom instruction.

From these first observations and our own research into children's book selection strategies, began a journey that would ultimately culminate in this book. During the course of this journey, we have learned from, shared ideas with, and worked shoulder-to-shoulder with hosts of classroom teachers, librarians, and other school professionals.

Now when we return to these schools we find classroom libraries that are the axis of teaching. We find pleasant, well-lit, designed and decorated classroom spaces with multiple bookshelves carefully arranged, leveled, and labeled. And, most gratifying of all, these areas pulse with student involvement. It has been a privilege to witness the growth and development of these classroom libraries from bulb to blossom.

In closing, let's remember that silence in the classroom should not automatically be equated with productive learning, In these pages we have acknowledged that the most valuable language-learning experiences often occur among students as they interact around reading material (Kasten, 1997). We have shared the belief that creating a social learning environment within the classroom can greatly enhance a student's language development (Vygotsky, 1978). We have recognized that encouraging students to discuss what they are reading on their own encourages motivation for reading (Koskinen, Palmer, Codling and Gambrell, 1994).

Our hope now is that what you have found in the pages of this book will help to give your own classroom library more teaching power, to enrich your instruction in every content subject, to motivate and engage your students to learn, and to improve reading achievement in your classrooms. We wish you well and invite you to share with us your journeys in giving your classroom libraries more teaching power!

Selected References

Allington, R.L. *What Really Matters for Struggling Readers: Designing Research-based Programs.* New York: Addison Wesley Longman, 2001.

Anderson, R. C., Wilson, P. T., and Fielding, L. G. "Growth in Reading and How Children Spend Their Time Outside of School." *Reading Research Quarterly* 23 (1988): 285–303.

Atwell, N. *In the Middle: Writing, Reading, and Learning With Adolescents.* Portsmouth, NH: Heinemann, 1987.

Austin, M.C., and Morrison, C. *The First R: The Harvard Report on Reading in Elementary Schools.* New York: Macmillan, 1963.

Baker, S.L. "Overload, Browers, and Selections." *Library and Information Science Research* 8 (1986): 315–319.

Barrentine, S. J. "Engaging With Reading Through Interactive Read Alouds." *The Reading Teacher* 50, no. 1 (1996): 36–43.

Barrett, F. L. *A Teacher's Guide to Shared Reading.* Richmond Hill, Ontario, Canada: Scholastic-TAB Publications, 1982.

Bissett, D. "The Amount and Effect of Recreational Reading in Selected Fifth-Grade Classes." Doctoral dissertation, Syracuse University, 1969.

Brown, H. and Cambourne, B. *Read and Retell: A Strategy for the Whole-Language/Natural Learning Classroom.* North Ryde, NSW: Methuen Australia, 1987.

Brown, R. "A Library Is More Fun If It's Yours!" *Media and Methods,* 50, no. 1 (1978): 94–96.

Butler, C. "When the Pleasurable is Measurable." *Language Arts* 57, no. 8 (1980): 882–885.

Calkins, L. M., and Harwayne, S. *The Writing Workshop: A World of Difference.* Portsmouth, NH: Heinemann Educational Books, 1987. Video.

Calkins, L. *The Art of Teaching Writing* (new ed.). Portsmouth, NH: Heinemann Educational Books, 1994

Campbell, R. *Read Alouds With Young Children.* Newark, DE: International Reading Association, 2001.

Clark, M. M. *Young Fluent Readers.* London: Heinemann Education, 1976.

Cooper, J. D. *Literacy: Helping Children Construct Meaning,* Third Edition. Boston, MA: Houghton Mifflin Company, 1997.

Daniels, H. *Literature Circles: Voice and Choice in the Student-Centered Classroom.* Portland, ME: Stenhouse Publishers, 1994

Darling-Hammond, L. *The Right to Learn: A Blueprint for Creating Schools That Work.* San Francisco: Jossey-Bass, 1997.

Donovan, C. A., Smolkin, L. B., and Lomax, R. G. "Beyond the Independent-Level Text: Considering the Reader-Text Match in First Graders' Self-Selections During Recreational Reading." *Reading Psychology: An International Quarterly* 21 (2000): 309–333.

Durkin, D. *Children Who Read Early: Two Longitudinal Studies.* New York: Teachers College Press, 1966.

Ehri, L. C., and Sweet, J. "Fingerpoint-Reading of Memorized Text: What Enables Beginners to Process the Print?" *Reading Research Quarterly* 26 (1991): 442–462.

Fischer, P. "The Reading Preference of Third-, Fourth-, and Fifth-graders." *Reading Horizons* 16 (1988): 62–70.

Fitzgerald, J. "English-as-a-Second-Language Learners' Cognitive Reading Processes: A Review of Research in the United States." *Review of Educational Research* 65 (1995): 145–190.

Fountas, I.C., and Pinnell, G.S. *Guided Reading: Good First Teaching for All Children.* Portsmouth, NH: Heinemann Educational Books, 1996.

Fountas, I.C., and Pinnell, G.S. *Leveled Books for Readers, Grades 3–6: A Companion Volume to Guiding Readers and Writers.* Portsmouth, NH: Heinemann Educational Books, 2001.

Fountas, I.C., and Pinnell, G.S. *Matching Books to Readers: Using Leveled Books in Guided Reading, K–3.* Portsmouth, NH: Heinemann Educational Books, 1999.

Fractor, J.S., Woodruff, M.C., Martinez, M. G, and Teale, W. H. "Let's Not Miss Opportunities to Promote Voluntary Reading: Classroom Libraries in the Elementary School." *The Reading Teacher* 46, (6) (1993): 476–484.

Freeman, Y.S., and Freeman, D. E. *Whole Language for Second Language Learners.* Portsmouth, NH: Heinemann Educational Books, 1992.

Gambrell, L. B. "Creating Classroom Cultures That Foster Reading Motivation." *The Reading Teacher* 50, no. 1 (1966): 14–25.

Gambrell, L. B. "It's Not Either/Or but More: Research Concerning Fictional and Nonfictional Reading Experiences to Improve Comprehension." Paper presented at the 46th Annual Convention of the International Reading Association, New Orleans, LA, April, 2001.

Gambrell, L. B., and Almasi, J. F. *Lively Discussions!: Fostering Engaged Reading.* Newark, DE: International Reading Association, 1996.

Goldenberg, C. "Making Schools Work for Low-Income Families in the 21st Century." *Handbook of Early Literacy Research,* eds. S. B. Neuman and D.K. Dickinson. New York: Guilford Press, 2001.

Hancock, J. and Hill, S. *Literature-Based Reading Programs at Work.* Portsmouth, NH: Heinemann Educational Books, 1998.

Hartman, D. K. "Eight Readers Reading: The Intertextual Links of Proficient Readers Reading Multiple Passages." *Reading Research Quarterly* 30 (1995): 520–561.

Hepler, S. "Creating a Classroom Library: Getting Started." *Learning* 92, 21, no. 2 (1992): 95–106.

Hiebert, E. H., Mervar, K.B., and Person, D. "Research Directions: Children's Selection of Trade Books in Libraries and Classrooms." *Language Arts* 67, (1990): 758–763.

Hoffman, J.V. Roser, N.L. and Battle, J. "Reading Aloud in Classrooms: From The Modal Toward the 'Model.'" *The Reading Teacher* 46, no. 6 (1993): 496–503.

Holdaway, D. "Shared Book Experience: Teaching Reading Using Favorite Books." *Theory Into Practice* 21 (1981): 293–300.

Holdaway, D. *The Foundations of Literacy.* Sydney, Australia: Ashton Scholastic, 1979.

Huck, C. *Children's Literature in the Elementary School,* Third Edition. New York: Holt, Rinehart and Winston, 1979.

Kasten, W. C. "Learning Is Noisy: The Myth of Silence in the Reading-Writing Classroom," 88–101. In *Peer Talk in the Classroom: Learning From Research,* J. R. Paratore and R. L. McCormack (eds.), Newark, DE: International Reading Association, 1997.

King, E. M. "Critical Appraisal of Research on Children's Reading Interest, Preferences, and Habits." *Canadian Education and Research Digest,* (December, 1967): 312–316.

Koskinen, P. S., Palmer, B. M., Codling, R. M., and Gambrell, L. B. (eds.). "In Their Own Words: What Elementary Students Have to Say About Motivation to Read." *The Reading Teacher* 48 (1994): 176–178.

Kotch, L. and Zackman, L. *The Author Studies Handbook, Grades K–8.* New York: Scholastic Inc., 1990.

Kurstedt, R. and Koutras, M. *Teaching Writing with Picture Books as Models.* NY: Scholastic Inc., 2000.

Mervar, K. B. *"Amount of Reading In and Out of School and Book-Selection Skills of Second-Grade Students in Textbook-Based and Literature-Based Programs."* Doctoral dissertation, University of Colorado, Boulder, 1989.

Mooney, M. E. *Reading to, With, and by Children.* Katonah, NY: Richard C. Owens, 1990.

Morrow, L. M. "Developing Young Voluntary Readers: The Home—the Child—the School." *Reading Research and Instruction* 25, no. 1 (1985): 1–8.

Morrow, L. M. "Relationships Between Literature Programs, Library Corner Designs, and Children's Use of Literature." *Journal of Educational Research* 76, Jul–Aug. (1982):339–44.

Morrow, L.M., and Simon, C. S. "Encouraging Voluntary Reading: The Impact of a Literature Program on Children's Use of Library Centers." *Reading Research Quarterly* 21, no. 3 (1986): 330–346.

National Institute of Child Health and Human Development. *Report of the National Reading Panel: Teaching Children to Read, an Evidence-based Assessment of the Scientific Research Literature on Reading and Its Implications for Reading Instruction* (NIH pub. NO. 00-4769). Washington, DC: U.S. Government Printing Office, 2000.

Neuman, S. B. *The Importance of Classroom Libraries*. New York: Scholastic, Inc., 2000.

Neuman, S.B. "Books Make a Difference: A Study of Access to Literacy." *Reading Research Quarterly* 34 (1999): 286–311.

Ohlhausen, M.M., and Jepsen, M. "Lessons from Goldilocks: 'Somebody's Been Choosing My Books but I Can Make My Own Choices Now!'" *New Advocate* 5, no. 1 (1992): 31–46.

Opitz, M.F. "Cultural Diversity + Supportive Text = Perfect Books for Beginning Readers." *The Reading Teacher*, 52, no. 8 (1999): 888–898.

Pang, V.O., Colvin, C., Tran, M., and Barba, R.H. "Beyond Chopsticks and Dragons: Selecting Asian-American Literature for Children." *The Reading Teacher*, 46, no. 3 (1992): 216–224.

Pilgreen, J. L. *The SSR Handbook: How to Organize and Manage a Sustained Silent Reading Program*. Portsmouth, NH: Heinemann Educational Books, 2000.

Pinnell, G.S., and Fountas, I.C *Leveled Books for Readers Grades 3–6: A Companion Volume to Guiding Readers and Writers*. Portsmouth, NH: Heinemann Educational Books, 2002.

Reutzel, D. R. (1995). "Fingerpoint-Reading and Beyond: Learning About Print Strategies (LAPS)." *Reading Horizons* 35, no. 4 (1995): 310–328.

Reutzel, D. R. and Fawson, P.C. "Using a Literature Webbing Strategy Lesson With Predictable Books." *The Reading Teacher* 43, no. 3 (1989): 208–215.

Reutzel, D. R., and Cooter, R. B., Jr. "Organizing for Effective Instruction: The Reading Workshop." *The Reading Teacher* 44, no. 8 (1991): 548–555.

Reutzel, D. R., and Cooter, R. B. *Teaching Children to Read: Putting the Pieces Together*, Third Edition. Upper Saddle River, NJ: Merrill/Prentice-Hall, 2000.

Reutzel, D. R., and Gali, K. "The Art of Children's Book Selection: A Labyrinth Unexplored." Paper presented at the International Reading Association Conference, Toronto, Canada, 1996.

Reutzel, D. R., and Gali, K. "The Art of Children's Book Selection: A Labyrinth Unexplored. *Reading Psychology* 19, no. 1 (1998): 3–50.

Robb, L. *Teaching Reading in Middle School*. NY: Scholastic Inc., 2000.

Rosenblatt, L. *"The Reader, the Text, the Poem."* Carbondale, IL: Southern Illinois Press, 1978.

Schulman, M.B. and Payne, C. D. *Guided Reading: Making It Work*. NY: Scholastic Inc., 2000.

Short, K.G., Harste, J. C. and Burke, C. *Creating Classrooms for Authors and Inquirers*. Second Edition. Portsmouth, NH: Heinemann Educational Books, 1995.

Siegel, M. "Reading as Signification." Doctoral dissertation. Indiana University, 1983.

Taylor, D. *Family Literacy: Young Children Learning to Read and Write*. Portsmouth, NH: Heinemann Educational Books, 1983.

Teale, W.H., and Martinez, M. "Teachers Reading to Their Students: Different Styles, Different Effects?" ERIC Document Reproduction Service. 269 754, 1986.

Timion, C. S. "Children's Book-Selection Strategies." *Reading and Writing Connections: Learning From Research*, eds. J. W. Irwin and M. A. Doyle. Newark, DE: International Reading Association, 1992.

Tobin, A. W. "A Multiple Discriminant Cross-Validation of the Factors Associated With the Development of Precocious Reading Achievement." Doctoral dissertation, University of Delaware, Newark, 1981.

Tunnell, M. O. and Jacobs, J. S. *Children's Literature, Briefly*. Upper Saddle River, NJ: Prentice-Hall, Inc, 2001.

Turner, J., and Paris, S. G. "How Literacy Tasks Influence Children's Motivation for Literacy." *The Reading Teacher* 48, no. 8 (1995): 662–673.

Veatch, J. (1968). *How to Teach Reading with Children's Books*. New York: Richard C. Owen.

Vygotsky, L. S. *Mind in Society: The Development of Higher Psychological Processes*. Cambridge, MA: Harvard University Press, 1978.

Wendelin, K. H. and Zinck, R. A. "How Students Make Book Choices." *Reading Horizons* 23, no.2 (1983): 84–88.

Worthy, J. "Removing Barriers to Voluntary Reading for Reluctant Readers: The Role of School and Classroom Libraries." *Language Arts* 73 (1996): 483–492.

Selected Children's Books

A is for Aloha. Feeney, S. Honolulu, HI: University of Hawaii Press, 1985.

A Jar of Dreams. Uchida, Y. New York: Atheneum, 1981.

A Picture Book of George Washington Carver. Adler, D. A. New York: Holiday House, 1999.

A Picture Book of Sitting Bull. Adler, D. New York: Holiday House, 1993.

A Pizza the Size of the Sun. Prelutsky, J. New York: Greenwillow Books, 1996.

A Racecourse for Andy. Wrightson, P. San Diego, CA: Harcourt, Brace & Co., 1968.

A River Dream. Say, A. New York: Houghton Mifflin, 1988.

A Wrinkle in Time. L'Engle, M. New York: Dial, 1962.

A Year Down Yonder. Peck, R. New York: Dial, 2000.

Action Alphabet. Rotner, S. New York: Atheneum, 1996.

Aesop's Fables. Kredel, F. New York: Grosset Pub., 1963.

Aesop's Fables. Holder, H. New York: Viking, 1981.

Aesop's Fables. Hague, M. New York: Henry Holt & Co., 1985.

Aesop's Fables. Pinkney, J. San Francisco, CA: Chronicle Books, 2000.

Alice With the Golden Hair. Hull, E. New York: Atheneum, 1981.

America: My Land, Your Land, Our Land. Nikola-Lisa, W. New York: Lee & Low, 1997.

Anansi Does the Impossible. Aardema, V. New York: Atheneum, 1997.

As Long as the Rivers Flow. Allen, P. G. and Smith, P. C. New York: Scholastic, Inc., 1996.

Asteroid Impact. Henderson, D. New York: Dial, 2000.

Athletic Shorts. Crutcher, C. New York: Greenwillow, 1991.

Author Talk: Conversations With Judy Blume, Bruce Brooks, Karen Cushman, Russell Freedman, Lee Bennett Hopkins, James Howe, Johanna Hurwitz, E. L. Konigsburg, Lois Lowry, Ann M. Martin, Nicholasa Mohr, Gary Paulsen, John Scieszka, Seymour Simon And Laurence Yep. Marcus, L. S. New York: Simon & Schuster, 2000.

Baseball, Football, Daddy, and Me. Friend, D. New York: Viking, 1990.

Be Good to Eddie Lee. Fleming, V. New York: Putnam, 1993.

Blizzard! The Storm That Changed America. Murphy, J. New York: Scholastic, Inc., 2000.

Brooklyn, Bugsy, and Me. Bowdish, L. New York: Farrar, Straus & Giroux, 2000.

Brown Bear, Brown Bear. Martin, B. New York: Henry Holt & Co., 1990.

Bunnicula: A Rabbit Tale of Mystery. Howe, D. and Howe, J. New York: Simon & Schuster, 1999.

Buttons. Cole, B. New York: Farrar, Straus & Giroux, 2000.

Cam Jansen and the Mystery of the Babe Ruth Baseball. Adler, D. New York: Scholastic. Inc., 1982.

Child of the Owl. Yep, L. New York: Harper and Row, 1977.

Children of the River. Crew, L. New York: Dell, 1989.

Clever Tortoise: A Traditional African Tale. Martin, F. Cambridge, MA: Candlewick, 2000.

Coconut Mon. Milstein, L. New York: Tambourine, 1995.

Commander Toad in Space. Yolen, J. New York: Coward, McCann & Geoghegan, 1980.

Crazy Lady. Conly, J. L. New York: HarperCollins, 1993.

Cumbaya. Cooper, F. New York: Morrow Junior Books, 1998.

Danger Guys on Ice. Abbott, T. New York: HarperCollins, 1995.

Dark Dreams. Rinaldo, C. L. New York: Harper and Row, 1974.

Dmitri the Astronaut. Agee, J. New York: HarperCollins, 1996.

Dragonwings. Yep, L. New York: Harper and Row, 1975.

Elephants Aloft. Baker, K. San Diego, CA: Harcourt, Brace & Co., 1993.

Emily's First 100 Days of School. Wells, R. New York: Hyperion, 2000.

Encyclopedia Brown: Boy Detective. Sobol, D. J. New York: Bantam Books, 1985.

Face-Off. Christopher, M. Boston, MA: Little, Brown & Co., Inc., 1972.

Falling Up. Silverstein, S. New York: HarperCollins, 1996.

Fatima and the Dream Thief. Schami, R. New York: North-South Books, 1996.

Favorite Nursery Tales. dePaola, T. New York: Putnam, 1986.

Feast for 10. Falwell, C. New York: Scholastic, Inc., 1993.

Fiesta!. Guy, G. F. New York: Greenwillow, 1996.

Fighting Tackle. Christopher, M. Boston, MA: Little, Brown & Co, Inc., 1995.

First Snow. Coutant, H. New York: Alfred A. Knopf, 1974.

First Your Penney. Hill, D. New York: Atheneum, 1985.

Fledgling. Blake, J. R. New York: Philomel, 2000.

For Love of Jody. Branscum, R. New York: Lothrop, 1979.

Freckle Juice. Blume, J. New York: Simon & Schuster, 1971.

Friends in the Park. Bunnett, R. Bellingham, WA: Our Kids Press, 1992.

Gershon's Monster: A Story for the Jewish New Year. Kimmel, E. A. New York: Scholastic, Inc., 2000.

Gorillas. Simon, S. New York: HarperCollins, 2000

Greetings, Sun. Gershator, P. and Gershator, D. New York: DK, 1998.

Hands! Kroll, V. Honesdale, PA: Boyds Mills, 1997.

Harry Potter and the Goblet of Fire. Rowling, J. K. New York: Scholastic, Inc., 2000.

Harry Potter and the Sorcerer's Stone. Rowling, J. K. New York: Scholastic, Inc., 1997.

Hau Kola = Hello Friend. Goble, P. Katonah, NY: Richard C. Owen, 1994.

Hog Music. Helldorfer, M. C. New York: Viking, 2000.

How Much is a Million? Schwartz, D. M. New York: Lothrop, Lee, and Shepherd Books, 1985.

How the Whale Became and Other Stories. Hughes, T. New York: Orchard, 2000.

How to Talk to Your Cat. George, J. C. New York: HarperCollins, 2000.

I Am Me! Brandenberg, A. San Diego, CA: Harcourt Brace & Co., 1996.

I'm the Big Sister Now. Emmert, M. Morton Grove, IL: Albert Whitman, 1989.

In My Own Time: Almost an Autobiography. Bawden, N. New York: Clarion, 1994.

In Real Life: Six Women Photographers. Sills, L. New York: Holiday House, Inc., 2000.

In the Night Kitchen. Sendak, M. New York: HarperCollins, 1970.

Into the A, B, Sea: An Ocean Alphabet. Rose, D. L. New York: Scholastic, Inc., 2000.

Is Underground. Aiken, J. New York: Delacorte, 1993.

Island of the Blue Dolphins. O'Dell, C. New York: Random House, 1978.

It's Too Late For Sorry. Hanlon, E. New York: Dell, 1978.

Jed's Junior Space Patrol. Marzollo, J. New York: Dial, 1982.

Joe DiMaggio. Appel, M. Broomall, PA: Chelsea House, 1990.

Journey to Topaz. Uchida, Y. New York: Charles Scribner's Sons, 1971.

Journey Home. Uchida, Y. New York: Atheneum, 1978.

Just Like Emma: How She Has Fun in God's World. Wright, C. Minneapolis, MN: Augsburg Fortress, 1993.

Just People and Other Poems for Young Readers; and Paper/Pen/Poem: A Young Writer's Way to Begin. Appelt, K. Spring, TX: Absey & Co., 1997.

Lester's Dog. Hesse, K. New York: Crown, 1993.

Lester's Turn. Slepian, J. New York: Macmillian, 1981.

Magic Money. Addler, D. New York: Random House, 1997.

Making Room for Uncle Joe. Litchfield, A. B. Morton Grove, IL: Whitman, 1984.

Malcolm X: A Fire Burning Brightly. Myers, W. D., New York: HarperCollins, 2000.

Mama Zooms. Cowen-Fletcher, J. New York: Scholastic, Inc., 1993.

Mammalabilia: Poems and Paintings. Florian, D. San Diego, CA: Harcourt, Brace & Co., 2000.

Mandy Sue's Day. Karim R. New York: Clarion Books, 1994.

Memories of Summer. White, R. New York: Farrar, Straus & Giroux, 2000.

Michelangelo. Stanley, D. New York: HarperCollins, 2000.

Misoso: Once Upon a Time Tales from Africa. Aardema, V. New York: Alfred A. Knopf, 1994.

More Rootabagas. Sandburg, C. New York: Alfred A. Knopf, 1993.

Mr. Popper's Penguins. Atwater, F., and Atwater, R. New York: Scholastic, Inc., 1994.

My America: A Poetry Atlas of the United States. Hopkins, L. B. New York: Simon & Schuster, 2000.

My Five Senses. Miller M. New York: Aladdin Paperbacks, 1998.

Naomi Knows It's Springtime. Kastner, J. Honesville, PA: Boyds Mills, 1993.

Nate the Great and the Mushy Valentine. Sharmat, M. W. New York: Young Yearling, 1995.

Navajo ABC: A Dine Alphabet. Tapahonso, L., New York: Simon & Schuster, 1995.

Never Fear, Flip the Dip is Here. Hanft, P. New York: Dial, 1991.

Night Fall. Aiken, J. New York: Dell, 1969.

No Mirrors in My Nana's House. Barnwell, Y. San Diego, CA: Harcourt, Brace & Co., 1998.

Norman Rockwell: Storyteller With a Brush. Gherman, B. New York: Atheneum, 2000.

Nory Ryan's Song. Giff, P. R. New York: Bantam, 2000.

Now I'm Big. Miller, M. New York: Greenwillow, 1996.

Olivia. Falconer, I. New York: Atheneum, 2000.

On the Bus With Joanna Cole. Saul, W. Portsmouth, NH: Heinemann, 1996.

Only One Cowry: A Dahomean Tale. Gershator, P. New York: Orchard, 2000.

Play. Morris, A. New York: Lothrop, 1998.

Polar Bear, Polar Bear. Martin, B. New York: Henry Holt & Co., 1991.

Rain. Stojic, M. New York: Crown, 2000.

Redwall. Jacques, B. New York: Philomel, 1986.

Risk 'n Roses. Slepian, J. New York: Philomel, 1990.

River Boy. Bowler, T. New York: Margaret McElderry, 2000.

Roll of Thunder, Hear My Cry. Taylor, M. D. New York: Puffin, 1997.

Samurai of Gold Hill. Uchida, Y. New York: Charles Scribner's Sons, 1972.

Sea Glass. Yep, L. New York: Harper and Row, 1979.

Seal Surfer. Foreman, M. San Diego, CA: Harcourt, Brace & Co., 1996.

Silent to the Bone. Konigsburg, E. L. New York: Atheneum, 2000.

Slow Dance Heart Break Blues. Adoff, A. New York: Lothrop, 1995.

Smoky Mountain Rose: An Appalachian Cinderella. Schroeder, A. New York: Dial, 1997.

Sniglets. Hall, R. New York: Macmillan, 1984.

Somewhere Today. Thomas, S. M. Morton Grove, IL: Albert Whitman, 1998.

Space Race. Waugh, S. New York: Delacorte, 2000.

Spyglass: An Autobiography. Deschamps, H. New York: Henry Holt & Co., 1995.

Stone Bench in an Empty Park. Janeczko, P. B. New York: Orchard, 2000.

Stowaway. Hesse, K. New York: Simon & Schuster, 2000.

Street Music: City Poems. Adoff, A. New York: HarperCollins, 1995.

Take Wing. Little, J. Boston, MA: Little, Brown & Co., Inc., 1968.

Ten Times Better. Michelson, R. Marshall Cavendish Corp., 2000.

The Alfred Summer. Slepian, J. New York: Macmillian, 1980.

The Amazing Life of Benjamin Franklin. Giblin, J. C. New York: Scholastic, Inc., 2000.

The Arabian Nights. Philip, N. New York: Orchard, 1994.

The Art of Eric Carle. Carle, E. New York: Putnam, 1996.

The Art of Keeping Cool. Lisle, J. T. New York: Atheneum, 2000.

The Baby Beebee Bird. Massie, D. R. New York: HarperCollins, 2000.

The Best Bad Thing. Uchida, Y. New York: Atheneum, 1982.

The Big Brown Box. Russo, M. New York: Greenwillow, 2000.

The Bridge to Terabithia. Paterson, K. New York: Thomas Y. Crowell, 1977.

The Bus People. Anderson, R. Hold, 1989.

The Door in the Wall. De Angeli, M. and De Angeli, T. New York: Yearling Books, 1990.

The Everlasting Hills. Hunt, I. New York: Scribner, 1985.

The Falcon's Wing. Buchanan, D. L. New York: Orchard, 1992.

The Fortune-Tellers. Alexander, L. New York: Dutton, 1992.

The Gift of the Crocodile: A Cinderella Story. Sierra, J. New York: Simon & Schuster, 2000.

The Giver. Lowry, L. Boston, MA: Houghton Mifflin, 1994.

The Golden Carp and Other Tales from Vietnam. Vuong, L. D. New York: Lothrop, 1993.

The Happiest Ending. Uchida, Y. New York: Atheneum, 1985.

The Hidden Forest. Baker, J. New York: Greenwillow, 2000.

The High King. Alexander, L. New York: Henry Holt & Co., 1968.

The Hunter: A Chinese Folktale. Casanova, M. New York: Atheneum, 2000.

The Invisible Thread. Uchida, Y. Englewood Cliffs, NJ: Julian Messner, 1991.

The Journey: Japanese Americans, Racism, and Renewal. Hamanaka, S. New York: Orchard, 1990.

The Little Golden Lamb. Greene, E. Boston, MA: Houghton Mifflin, 2000.

The Lost Garden: A Memoir. Yep, L. Englewood Cliffs, NJ: Julian Messner, 1991.

The Man Who Loved Clowns. Wood, J. R. New York: Putnam, 1992.

The Night Worker. Banks, K. Frances Foster Books, 2000.

The Palm of My Heart: Poetry by African American Children. Adedjouma, D. Madison, WI: Turtleback Books, 1996.

The Raft. LaMarche, J. New York: HarperCollins, 2000.

The Secret Footprints. Alvarez, J. New York: Knopf, 2000.

The Serpent Slayer and Other Stories of Strong Women. Tchana, K. Boston, MA: Little, Brown & Co, Inc., 2000.

The Star Fisher. Yep, L. New York: Morrow Books, 1991.

The Steadfast Tin Soldier. Lynch, P. J. San Diego, CA: Harcourt Brace & Co., 1992.

The Stupids Die. Allard, H. Boston, MA: Houghton Mifflin, 1985.

The Summer of the Swans. Byars, B. New York: Viking, 1970.

The Trojan Horse: How the Greeks Won the War. Little, E. New York: Random House, 1988.

The Very Hungry Caterpillar. Carle, E. New York: Philomel, 1969.

The Wolves of Willoughby Chase. Aiken, J. New York: Doubleday, 1963.

Thomas Alva Edison: Great Inventor. Adler, D. A. New York: Holiday, 1990.

Thy Friend Obadiah. Turkle, B. New York: Viking, 1982.

Tikki, Tikki, Tembo. Mosel, A. New York: Henry Holt & Co., 1968.

Toby. Talbert, M. New York: Dial, 1987.

Too Much Noise. McGovern, A. Boston, MA: Houghton Mifflin, 1967.

Torn Thread. Isaacs, A. New York: Scholastic, Inc., 2000.

Tortillas and Lullabies/Tortillas y Cancioncitas. Reiser, L. New York: Greenwillow, 1998.

True Lies: 18 Tales for You to Judge. Shannon, G. New York: Greenwillow, 1997.

Umbrella. Yashima, T. New York: Viking, 1958.

Uno, Dos, Tres; One, Two, Three. Mora, P. New York: Clarion, 1996.

Uptown. Collier, B. New York: Henry Holt & Co., 2000.

Wake Up House! A Room Full of Poems. Lillegard, D. New York: Simon & Schuster, 2000.

Watership Down. Adams, R. New York: Macmillan, 1972.

We're Going on a Bear Hunt. Rosen, M. New York: Macmillian, 1989.

Welcome Home, Jellybean. Shyer, M. F. New York: Macmillian, 1978.

When I First Came to This Land. Ziefert, H. New York: Putnam, 1998.

When Jessie Came Across the Sea. Hest, A. and Lynch P. J. Cambridge, MA: Candlewick Press, 1997.

Where's Chimpy? Rabe, B. Morton Grove, IL: Albert Whitman, 1988.

Whoever You Are. Fox, M., San Diego, CA: Harcourt, 1997.

Whose Hat? Miller, M. New York: Mulberry Paperback, 1997.

Why Mosquitoes Buzz in People's Ears: A West African Tale. Aardema, V. New York: Dial, 1975.

Wingman. Pinkwater, M. New York: Dell, 1975.

Wish On a Unicorn. Hesse, K. New York: Henry Holt & Co., 1991.

With the Wind. Damrell, L. New York: Orchard, 1991.

Work. Morris, A. New York: Lothrop, 1998.

Take the Lead

Leads are the first words that you read when you begin a book. They are written to get your attention and keep you reading. Authors use different kinds of leads. There are five kinds described below. In your independent reading, look for an example of each of the different kinds of leads, Write the lead line(s) you find in their appropriate category and the book's title in the next column. An example is given for each category.

Kind of Lead	Lead Lines	Book Title
SETTING LEAD (tells where or when the story takes place)	Ex: My great-aunt Arizona was born in a log cabin her papa built in the meadow on Henson Creek in the Blue Ridge Mountains.	*My Great Aunt Arizona* by Gloria Houston
CHARACTER LEAD (describes the character)	Ex: Mrs. Gorf had a long tongue and pointed ears.	*Sideways Stories From Wayside School* by Louis Sachar
DIALOGUE LEAD (someone's talking)	Ex: "Where's Papa going with that ax?"	*Charlotte's Web* by E. B. White

Kind of Lead	Lead Lines	Book Title
ACTION LEAD (something's happening)	Ex: Walking back to camp through the swamp, Sam wondered whether to tell his father what he had seen.	*The Trumpet of the Swan* by E. B. White
SUMMARY LEAD (answers who, what, where, when, or why)	Ex: David often wondered about how he happened to be sitting there on the stair landing, within arm's reach of the headlesss cupid, at the very moment when his stepmother left Westerly House to bring Amanda home.	*The Headless Cupid* by Zilpha Keatley Snyder

Which kind of lead do you think is most effective?

_____

_____

Which lead made you want to read the book?

_____

_____

—From *Keep the Rest of the Class Reading and Writing … While You Teach Small Groups* by Susan Finney (Scholastic Professional Books, 2000)

Name_____ Date_____

Checklist for Monitoring Independent Reading

Observations	Teacher's Notes
BOOK LOG ENTRIES	
Number of books	
Variety of titles	
INDEPENDENT READING	
Selects books on independent level	
Gets started quickly	
Self-helps before seeking peer or teacher assistance	
Shows pleasure in reading through journal entries, talk, and projects	
WRITTEN WORK	
Book review	
Critical paragraphs, essays	
Projects	
Dialogue journals	
ORAL WORK	
Book talk, reviews	
Reading fluency	
Oral reading error patterns	
ADDITIONAL NOTES AND QUESTIONS:	

—From *35 Must-Have Assessment & Record-Keeping Forms for Reading* by Laura Robb
(Scholastic Professional Books, 2001)

STUDENT REFLECTION FORM

Name________________________________ Date______________________________

When I Write in My Reading Notebook

I think of interesting ideas and questions to write about.

- I make predictions.
- I write my opinions about some parts I didn't understand.
- I connect what I read to something that happened to me.
- I copy a particular line or phrase that I thought was well-written.
- I compare stories and characters.
- I tell why I chose a book or abandoned a book.
- I tell about some writing techniques I learned from the author that I want to try in my own stories.

I show that I understand literary elements.
(plot, setting, character development, and theme)

- I describe a character's traits (selfish, helpful, shy, friendly, and so on) and give examples from the story that back up my opinions.
- I tell how a character changed and give reasons for the change.
- I describe the story's problem and its resolution.
- I describe the story's setting (where and when it took place).
- I write about the story's theme (main idea or author's message).

I describe the writing styles of authors.

- I tell what I like about the way an author writes.
- I compare books by different authors.
- I copy the author's descriptions that put pictures (imagery) in my mind.
- I quote lines from a story that show how the author writes.

I tell about myself as a reader.

- I write about my favorite books and authors.
- I describe my childhood memories of stories.
- I write about an experience I had in a library, a bookstore, or a book fair.
- I write about the ways I've changed as a reader.
- I write about my reading habits—where, when, and how I like to read.
- I write about people—family, friends, teachers—who influenced my reading.

— From *40 Rubrics & Checklists to Assess Reading and Writing* by Adele Fiderer (Scholastic Professional Books, 1999)

Name_____ Date_____

Peer Book Conference

Our conference was on _____ **between:**
(date)

Name: _____

Name: _____

Title and Author: _____

Check the focus of the conference:

_____ Retelling of a chapter or the entire story

_____ The main character's changes from beginning to end

_____ Problems the main character faced and how he or she dealt with them

_____ Conflicts and resolutions

_____ The character and/or situations the reader connects to, and why

_____ Discussion of the genre and the genre's structure

_____ Questions(s) (note the questions(s) discussed)

_____ Visualizing parts of the story

_____ Confirming and adjusting predictions

_____ Discussion of new information and new words the reader met

_____ The illustrations

_____ The settings

_____ Reactions to the ending or other parts of the book

Preparation checklist:

_____ I came with my book.

_____ I brought my pencil.

List the main points of the discussion:

_____

_____

_____

_____

— From *35 Must-Have Assessment & Record-Keeping Forms for Reading* by Laura Robb (Scholastic Professional Books, 2001)

What a Character!

Book Title: _____

Character's Name: _____

Circle six of the character traits listed below that you think best describe the character you've named. On a separate sheet of paper, define each trait. Below each definition write a sentence that uses the word and explains why it describes the character. (An example from the book *Frindle* by Andrew Clements would be: Nick was **inventive** when he created a new word for a pen.) Staple this sheet to the page with your sentences.

angry	healthy	loyal	sensible
anguished	helpful	methodical	serious
contemplative	honest	modest	sincere
energetic	hopeful	motivated	sociable
enthusiastic	humble	open-minded	spontaneous
fair	humorous	optimistic	strong-willed
firm	imaginative	practical	stubborn
flexible	individualistic	purposeful	tenacious
forgiving	independent	prudent	thorough
frank	industrious	realistic	trustworthy
friendly	inventive	resourceful	untrustworthy
generous	kind	responsible	wary
gentle	likable	self-confident	witty
good-natured	logical	self-deluded	wretched

— From *35 Must-Have Assessment & Record-Keeping Forms for Reading* by Laura Robb (Scholastic Professional Books, 2001)